Introduction

Whether you have big experience with this needlecraft or less than a little, **The Big Book of Little Ribbon Embroidery Designs** will liberate the artist within you with its spectrum of 101 graceful motifs. Deanna Hall West's love of nature harmonizes beautifully with her passion for ribbon embroidery to deliver this assortment of designs featuring flowers, animals, fruit, vegetables, seashells, insects, and holiday scenes.

Proving the adage about big things and little packages, each motif is a mere two inches square (or smaller!), and is shown full-size in both the photograph and stitching guide in this book. Some designs are perfect for borders, others make lovely vignettes; still others are cleverly housed in shadowboxes we've named *Whatnots*. Many of the designs are coordinated for grouping, including the *Dutch Tile* set, *Symphony of Roses*, and an array of congruous shapes and themes from fanciful to fine.

As you envision your linens, clothing, and walls adorned with your favorite enchanting little scenes, be assured this book will teach you everything you'll need to know to coax and cajole a length of ribbon into a work of art. You'll marvel at your newfound wizardry as the ribbon twists and bends in compliance with your expressive, personal s' and these designs become your own. And your friend And your daughter's. And your Aunt Mildred's....

Contents

Ribbon Embroidery Basics

Supplies

Ribbon

Ribbons used for embroidery are chosen for their special properties. They must drape nicely and be able to be pulled through fabric without damage to the ribbon or the fabric. Silk ribbon is the preferred choice for embroidery, although some synthetics are available.

For ribbon embroidery, 4mm is the most commonly used width. Many of our designs also use 7mm ribbon, although the color range of 7mm is more limited than that of 4mm. Ribbon is usually packaged as a single solid color, but is also available in variegated form—where color values change along the length of the ribbon. The new sheer organdy ribbons can also be used (e.g., Bee & Flowers on page 14), available in slightly different widths than typical embroidery ribbon. If desired, a similar width and color of silk ribbon can be substituted for organdy ribbon in these designs. Mixing ribbon widths and styles adds to the textural contrast which is a strong aspect of this embroidery.

The Stitching Guides, beginning on page 13, list the ribbon colors to be used for each design. Refer to the Ribbon Color Conversion Key on page 61 for suggestions when using YLI or Bucilla brands of ribbon. Work with ribbon cut into 10"-12" (or shorter) pieces. Embroidery ribbons are relatively fragile, and during stitching the ribbon can be easily frayed. Short lengths help to prevent any damage.

Threads

Cotton embroidery floss is often used with ribbon to create narrow lines of embroidery, tack down a portion of a stitch, or preserve a special shape. When floss is required in a design, a generic color name is listed for the floss, usually to match the ribbon with which it is used. You can also use any of the following embroidery threads successfully:

Rayon, six-strand floss
Silk, six- or seven-strand floss
Crewel yarn, very fine wool
Floche, five-ply cotton
Flower thread, twisted matte-finish cotton
Marlitt, or similar-weight rayon thread
Pearl cotton, size 12 or 8

A "blended" color combines two thread color values to produce a new shade. When floss blend is noted in the Stitching Guides with the names of two colors—use one strand of each. Metallic gold thread is occasionally used to add sparkle to a design. Choose a fine braid, cord, or stranded metallic, and use the number of strands directed by the manufacturer.

Needles

Basically, three types of needles are used for ribbon embroidery: chenille, tapestry, and crewel. We find that all kinds have their place. Choose a sharp chenille needle or a blunt tapestry needle for ribbon stitching, a tapestry needle for embroidery floss, and a crewel needle for other fine threads.

One important factor to consider when choosing the correct needle is the size of the eye. With silk ribbon the needle's eye should be large enough for the ribbon to pass through easily, with little or no gathering. Also, the size of the needle's shaft needs to be large enough that a sufficient hole is made in the background fabric to accommodate the ribbon as it passes through the fabric without causing too much friction and damage to the ribbon. In sizing, the higher the number, the smaller the needle.

A chenille needle is a large sharp needle with a large eye. Sizes 18-22 are used for most embroidery with 4mm- and 7mm-wide ribbon.

A tapestry needle, with a blunt tip, of a size equivalent to the sharp chenille needle can also be used and you will avoid piercing threads of the background fabric or any of the stitching ribbon. Use a size 26 tapestry needle for cotton embroidery floss and a fine (size 28) tapestry needle or special beading needle to attach beads.

A crewel needle is a fine sharp needle with a large eye. This needle style is appropriate when embellishing a ribbon design with floss, silk thread, or any of the other accessory threads. The needle size (8, 9, or 10) will depend on the thread size and the number of strands used.

Fabrics

Any fabric with a medium weave will work as a background fabric. Knitted fabrics are often too loose to hold ribbon embroidery securely, but can be used if a lightweight non-stretch backing fabric is attached. Some fabric suggestions are:

Dressmaking fabrics—cotton, voile, silk, batiste, faille, moiré

Evenweave embroidery fabrics—plain weaves like linen, cottage cloth, Jobelan®, Lugana, or complex weaves like Aida and hardanger

Linen twill—often used for crewel embroidery

Specially-packaged ribbon embroidery fabric

For ribbon-embellished clothing, choose a fabric that does not require much ironing. A lightweight interfacing can be attached to the back of the fabric to prevent puckering around the embroidery. The garment needs to be laundered according to the ribbon manufacturer's washing instructions.

The back of ribbon embroidery is certainly not neat! When working on a ready-made garment, partially remove the lining to do the embroidery, then replace the lining, covering the back of the work. If there is no lining, consider attaching a soft material to the wrong side of the stitched area.

Scissors

Small, sharp embroidery scissors are needed. Besides cutting the ribbon and embroidery threads, the flat surface of the blade used in a stroking manner can help to spread the ribbon where it emerges from the fabric.

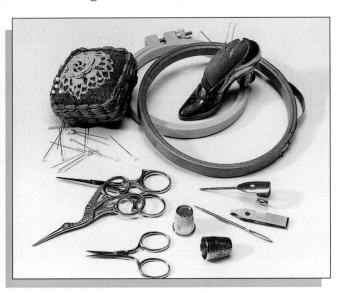

Frames and Hoops

The best ribbon embroidery results are achieved when the background fabric is held under tension during the stitching process. Use an appropriately sized embroidery hoop (especially when working on clothing) or needlework stretcher bars. If previously worked stitching needs to be held in place while working new stitches, use a small hoop, holding completed stitches with one hand while stitching with the other.

Additional Handy Tools

The following tools and supplies are helpful in creating a beautifully finished project:

Water-soluble marking pens or transfer pencils—to transfer a design to a light background fabric; use a light pen or pencil for dark fabrics.

Water-soluble fabric stabilizer—on which a design is traced, attached to background fabric, and later removed with water.

Trolley needle—to manipulate, spread, and adjust the ribbon.

Cotton swab (lightly moistened)—to remove any water-soluble marks on the fabric that are not covered by embroidery.

Stilletto, awl, or large-diameter needle—to puncture holes into tightly woven fabric, preventing wide ribbon from being damaged.

A soft handkerchief or facial tissue—to cover stitching that might be distorted by a hoop.

Small crochet hook—to pull ribbon ends under stitching and tidy up back of work.

Stitching Tips

- Work with short ribbon lengths (10" - 12") to prevent excessive ribbon damage.

- Keep ribbon untwisted on back of fabric; this makes it easier to spread out the stitches on the front of the fabric. If your ribbon comes up through the fabric looking twisty, turn to the wrong side and straighten ribbon as needed.

- Use thumb (or thumbnail) and forefinger of your non-stitching hand to hold previous work in place while working an adjacent stitch.

- Don't carry ribbon from one area to the next as you stitch. It might show through on the front, and as you stitch other colors in those areas, the carried ribbon might get in the way.

- When working with two (or more) threaded needles at the same time, bring the idle needle to rest temporarily on the front of the fabric, parking it away from the working area.

- To remove anchored ribbon from the needle's eye, gently pull on the short pierced end to loosen the knot, then pull ribbon off needle.

Special Techniques

Marking a Design on Fabric

You may work any design in a free-form manner, or draw a design outline directly on the background fabric. Place fabric directly over the design and trace with a water-soluble fabric-marking pen. If the fabric is heavy, a lightbox will be helpful. You can also use a #2 lead pencil (for light to medium-colored fabrics) or a white pencil (for dark fabrics).

Ribbon embroidery can also be worked with just position marks on the fabric, rather than a full pattern. This approach works especially well for a stem or branch. Draw the basic stem lines, then locations for the intended leaves, and stitch accordingly.

Threading the Needle

Thread ribbon end through the eye, and pull it through beyond tip of needle. Pierce the ribbon end with the needle, **Fig 1**. Holding point of needle, pull the long end of the ribbon to secure it.

Fig 1

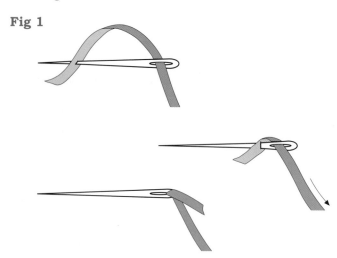

Making a Knot

To begin stitching, make this special knot, **Fig 2**, at end of ribbon. Drape ribbon end over needle; wrap working ribbon once around needle, then pull needle through the wrap to form a knot. When you begin to stitch, be careful not to pull too tightly, or the knot may come through the fabric.

Fig 2

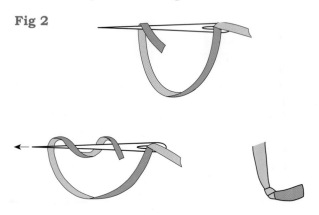

Ending the Ribbon

When you finish using a color, run the needle under a few stitches on the wrong side. The ribbon should end, whenever possible, toward the center of the stitching area to avoid being visible beyond the edge of the embroidery. If desired, pierce through some ribbon on the back before cutting the end, but make sure this does not disturb the front of your work. For added security, use floss or thread to tack ends together on back of work.

Using the Designs

These designs have been planned using primarily 4mm and 7mm ribbons, but occasionally organdy ribbons of different widths are used. Refer to the covers and color pages to choose the design(s) you want to stitch. The Stitching Guides for the designs are given in alphabetical order beginning on page 13. The Guides and the stitched designs on the covers and color pages 17-20 are shown actual size so you can match the size as you work.

A design can be enlarged or reduced if you remember the ribbon width limitations. To enlarge, add more stitches or change to a wider ribbon, whichever looks best. To reduce, use a narrower ribbon or take smaller (or fewer) stitches and/or pull the stitches more tightly. Always test-stitch the new size on scrap fabric before using it in a design. Ribbon embroidery is a technique that allows quite a bit of freedom with scale. It is perfectly fine to have an apple that is as large as a balloon. Of greater importance is the visual effect; it should be pleasing to the eye rather than a realistic size. And if you wish to work with different colors than we have chosen, feel free to do so.

Finishing Considerations

If your piece was worked on a frame, there will probably be no blocking required. If the finished embroidery is to be washed, pre-test the ribbon to make sure it is colorfast. Dip a small piece in water and place on a paper towel; let dry and check to see if the dye runs. If the ribbon is not colorfast, but the item must be washed, choose another ribbon. If you must wash, use cold water with mild soap and a cold water rinse.

When working on a ready-made garment, take into account the surface fabric needs as well as the embroidery. If you must take an iron to it, press face down on a thick padded surface—a terry cotton towel is an excellent choice—only lightly pressing the areas of stitching. Use caution to prevent scorching.

When framing, you may wish to protect the embroidery with glass. Because of the textural quality, choose a shadow box frame or insert spacers to keep the glass from touching the stitches.

Ribbon Embroidery Stitches

The stitch diagrams are shown using ribbon. When stitching with embroidery floss, use the same method and, unless otherwise directed, use two strands of floss.

When working any stitch, bring ribbon (or floss) up from back to front of fabric at odd (1, 3, 5) numbers and stitch down through fabric at even (2, 4, 6) numbers unless otherwise directed. Secondary stitching is labelled with sequential letters (A, B, C, etcetera).

Some designs have stitches in a random color arrangement. The Stitching Guide label will list all the colors used; the location of each color is your choice.

The stitches (numbers include their variations) are in the following alphabetical order:

Backstitches (2)	Ribbon Stitches (8)
Bead Stitch	Satin Stitch
Colonial Knot	Spider Web
Couching	Spiral Rose
Feather Stitch	Stem Stitch
French Knot	Straight Stitches (6)
Lazy Daisy Stitches (3)	Tack Stitch
Loop Stitches (2)	Weaving
Pin Stitch	Wrapped Bar

Backstitches

Backstitch

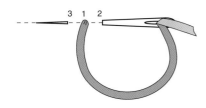

Bring needle up at 1, a stitch length away from beginning of design line. Stitch back down at 2, at beginning of line. Bring needle up at 3, then stitch back down to meet previous stitch (same hole as 1). Continue, carrying ribbon forward beneath fabric and stitching backward on the surface to meet previous stitch. Backstitch can be worked along curving or straight lines.

Wrapped Backstitch

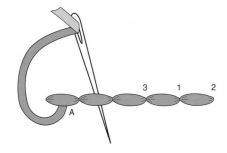

Work a row of Backstitch (above). Bring ribbon up at A, below last Backstitch and proceed to wrap each consecutive Backstitch once or twice by slipping needle beneath Backstitch, but not piercing the fabric. Stitch down into fabric to end.

Bead Stitch

Seed beads are attached using one strand of floss, usually to match the color of the bead. Thread floss into a needle and knot the end. Bring floss from back to front of fabric, slip on bead, and stitch back down. Knot floss on back. A string of beads (variation) can be attached in a similar manner. Bring knotted floss to front, slip on several beads, then stitch down to anchor string in desired position. Our stitched designs use Mill Hill seed beads.

Colonial Knot

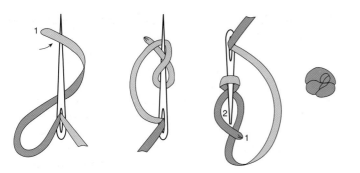

This makes a larger knot than the French Knot (page 7). Bring ribbon up at 1. Swing ribbon in a clockwise loop; follow arrow and slip point of needle beneath ribbon from left to right. Bring working ribbon around point of needle in a figure eight motion. Insert needle at 2, near 1; needle will be vertical. Pull ribbon loosely around needle as you pull needle through to back of fabric. Do not pull too tightly.

Couching

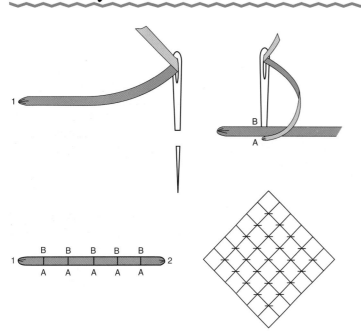

This technique requires one ribbon laid on the fabric and a second ribbon (or floss) to hold the first ribbon in place. Bring needle and ribbon up at 1, the left side of outline to be couched. Pull ribbon through, along intended couched position, and park it temporarily at right side of fabric.

Hold first ribbon flat and bring second needle with ribbon (or floss) up at A, below flat ribbon. Stitch down above flat ribbon (B), making a vertical stitch. Proceed to next couching point and repeat. At end of row, pass flat ribbon needle through to back of fabric (2) and secure it.

Couching can also be worked diagonally with parallel rows of ribbon or floss; each intersection is couched down with floss, forming a pattern.

Feather Stitch

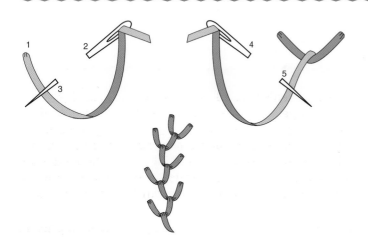

Bring needle up at 1. Swing ribbon to the right and straighten any twists in the ribbon. Insert needle at 2 and come up at 3, keeping loop below point of needle; pull until a "V" of proper tension appears.

Swing ribbon to the left and stitch down at 4 and up at 5; pull through. Swing ribbon to the right and repeat first "V" shape. Continue in this manner, moving from side to side or as the pattern indicates.

6

French Knot

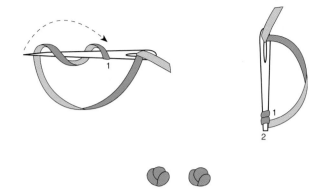

Bring needle up at 1 and wrap ribbon once or twice around shaft of needle. Swing point of needle clockwise and insert into fabric at 2, close to 1. Keep the working ribbon wrapped loosely around needle as you pull needle through to back of fabric. Release wrapping ribbon as knot is formed, and do not pull the knot too tightly. You can change the size of the French Knot by using different ribbon widths, wrapping the ribbon one or more times around needle, and/or varying your tension. To make a larger knot, refer to Colonial Knot (page 6). With floss, you can also make a larger knot by using more strands in the needle.

Lazy Daisy Stitches

Lazy Daisy Stitch

Bring needle up at 1 and re-insert needle at 2, next to 1 (skipping a thread or two to avoid piercing the ribbon). Pull until the loop is desired length. Bring needle up at 3 with loop below point of needle. Pull ribbon through until desired shape is formed. Re-insert needle over the loop at 4 (close to 3) to anchor it.

Modified Lazy Daisy Stitch

Using a wide ribbon, begin as for a Lazy Daisy Stitch (above), coming up at 1 and down at 2. Pull ribbon just enough to make a folded point. Use matching floss to tack point (A) in place and continue tacking to create desired shape. End off ribbon.

Open Lazy Daisy Stitch

This is worked in the same manner as a Lazy Daisy Stitch; however, instead of 1 and 2 being close together, they are a distance apart. This distance can vary, depending on the desired result.

Loop Stitches

Loop Stitch

 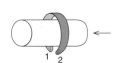

Bring needle up at 1, stitch down at 2, and pull ribbon part way through fabric. Insert a piece of drinking straw (or pencil, large tapestry needle, paper clip, etc.) through loop; pull ribbon snug to hold shape. Keep straw in place until the next loop is made in the same manner, then remove straw. If desired, these upright loops can be tacked in place.

(continued on page 8)

7

(continued from page 7)

Modified Loop Stitch

Use a wide ribbon to make a Loop Stitch (page 7). Push top of loop to fabric surface. Work a French Knot (page 7), Colonial Knot (page 6), or Bead Stitch (page 5) at center to hold loop in place.

Pin Stitch

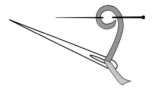

Using a long straight pin take a $1/8$" bite into background fabric. Bring ribbon-threaded needle up through fabric next to pin; wind ribbon around pin until desired size is reached. Stitch down to end. Using a single strand of floss to match ribbon, tack down opposite sides of coil. Remove pin.

If desired, work a Colonial or French Knot at center.

Ribbon Stitches

Ribbon Stitch

Bring needle up at 1 and flatten ribbon as it emerges through fabric. Extend ribbon just beyond length of stitch and insert needle through top of ribbon at 2. Pull ribbon gently through fabric as the sides of ribbon curl inward to form a point. Leave the curls showing by not pulling too tightly. Vary this stitch by using different ribbon widths and tension.

Modified Ribbon Stitch I

This technique creates a Ribbon Stitch with a straight horizontal base. Bring ribbon out of fabric above intended bottom edge of stitch (1). Hold ribbon downward and use matching floss to tack each side to fabric (A and B). Bring ribbon upward and stitch down (2) to work remainder of the Ribbon Stitch in the usual manner; dotted line shows hidden beginning section of ribbon.

Modified Ribbon Stitch II

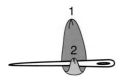

Begin as if to work a Ribbon Stitch (1-2), but do not pull ribbon completely through. Insert a large tapestry needle into the ribbon tunnel, then pull ribbon against needle only until a "roll" appears at the end of the stitch. Remove needle. If pulled too tightly, the usual curves will appear at the end instead of the roll.

Padded Ribbon Stitch

Make a Colonial Knot (page 6) or a French Knot (page 7), then make a Ribbon Stitch (page 8) centered over knot. The covered shape is shown by dotted lines. In the Stitching Guides, beginning on page 13, the stitching order lists the covered stitch. If desired, silk ribbon can be used for the covered stitch and organdy ribbon for the top stitch.

Twisted Ribbon Stitch

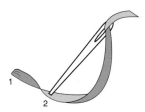

Begin at 1 as if to make a Ribbon Stitch (page 8), but give the ribbon a single twist before stitching down at 2 to create the point.

Modified Twisted Ribbon Stitch

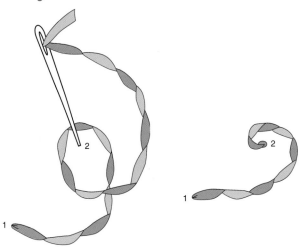

This forms a curving twisted petal with a knob at the tip. Begin as for Spiral Rose, page 10, and bring ribbon up at base of petal (1) and twist ribbon in a clockwise direction; swing twisted ribbon in a counterclockwise direction to form a loop. Hold loop in place; stitch down inside loop where end of petal will be (2). Slowly pull needle and ribbon through fabric until small spiral knot is formed at end. Use matching floss to tack petal in place if needed.

The shape can be reversed by working this stitch in the opposite direction. Twist ribbon counter-clockwise then make a clockwise loop.

Side Ribbon Stitch

Begin at 1 as if to make a Ribbon Stitch (page 8), but insert needle close to one edge of ribbon at 2. Continue to pull gently until desired shape for tip is achieved.

Padded Side Ribbon Stitch

Make a Colonial Knot (page 6) or a French Knot (page 7), then make a Side Ribbon Stitch (above) centered over knot. See Padded Ribbon Stitch for additional information.

Satin Stitch

This is a series of parallel Straight Stitches worked close to each other to fill a shape. Bring needle up at 1, down at 2, up at 3, etc. to fill shape. Use your non-stitching hand to flatten ribbon as you bring needle down at end of each stitch.

Spider Web

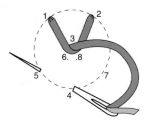

Create a base for weaving with ribbon (or floss). Bring needle up at 1, down at 2, and up at 3 with loop beneath needle's point; pull through. Stitch down at 4. Add two more legs (5-6 and 7-8). End off ribbon. Bring a different ribbon up at center of web and begin weaving over and under the five legs in a circular manner until desired fullness is achieved. To end, insert needle beneath web and pull gently through fabric. Do not worry about twists—they add interest and dimension.

If the flower includes a French or Colonial Knot at its center, begin weaving slightly away from center, leaving room for the knotted stitch.

In the Stitching Guides, beginning on page 13, the label lists the floss color used for the base and the ribbon color for weaving; if two ribbon colors are used, the color closest to center is noted (inside) and the other is noted (outside).

Spiral Rose

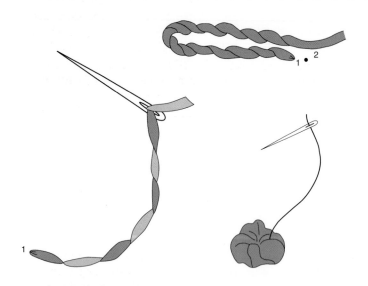

Bring ribbon up at 1, the planned center of the rose. Twist ribbon until entire length is tightly twisted. Form the twisted strand into a 1" or 1 1/4" loop and hold it close to fabric with your non-stitching thumb. Let the remaining ribbon (toward needle) untwist. Stitch down at 2, close to 1, and pull through to base of loop. Release loop and let it begin to untwist while pulling needle through to back; the ribbon will coil in upon itself to form a rose. Do not pull too tightly. Use matching floss to tack rose in place.

Stem Stitch

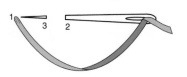

Bring needle up at 1. Use the thumb of your non-stitching hand to hold ribbon flat. Stitch down at 2 and up at 3, then pull the ribbon through. Continue in this manner, with ribbon held below stitching. Floss is often used to work this stitch.

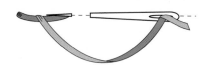

Straight Stitches

Straight Stitch

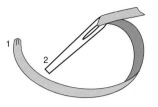

Bring needle from back of fabric at beginning point of stitch (1). Use non-stitching thumb and forefinger to keep ribbon from twisting as you stitch down at opposite end of stitch (2). Pull gently from 1 to 2, keeping the stitch flat.

Bent Straight Stitch

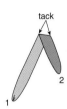

This technique is usually used for a leaf (or petal). Bring ribbon up at base of leaf (1). Use matching floss to tack leaf to fabric the desired distance from base; fold ribbon forward (hiding the tacking stitch) and enter fabric at desired location (2) for tip of leaf.

Modified Straight Stitch

This technique creates a Straight Stitch with a straight end. Bring ribbon out of fabric above intended bottom edge of stitch (1). Hold ribbon downward and use matching floss to tack each side to fabric (A and B). Bring ribbon upward and stitch down below intended top of stitch (2). Hold ribbon flat and use matching floss to tack each side down to fabric (C and D). Dotted lines show hidden beginning and ending sections of ribbon. If only one straight end is required, just the beginning of the Modified Straight Stitch is tacked down; stitch down into fabric at opposite end. These stitches can also be padded (see below).

Padded Straight Stitch

Make a Straight Stitch, then work a longer Straight Stitch directly over the first one.

The covered stitch can also be a Colonial or French Knot; the shape is shown by dotted lines beneath the top stitch. On the Stitching Guides, beginning on page 13, the stitching order lists the covered stitch. If desired, silk ribbon can be used for the covered stitch and organdy ribbon for the top stitch. Also, if a special shape is required for the top stitch, use matching floss to tack the edges in place.

Twisted Straight Stitch

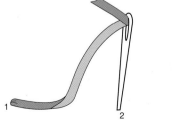

Bring needle up at 1, give ribbon a single twist, and stitch down at 2.

Modified Twisted Straight Stitch

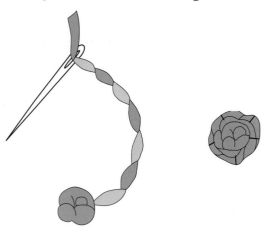

Begin stitch with a Colonial Knot (page 6) or French Knot (page 7). Bring ribbon up next to knot. Twist ribbon tightly and coil around central knot. Use contrasting floss to Couch (page 6) coil in place at regular intervals. When coil is desired size, stitch down to end.

Tack Stitch

Tacking is a technique that invisibly anchors the ribbon in a desired position. Use one strand of floss to match the ribbon. Make one or more tiny straight stitches along edge of ribbon to create an indentation or retain a shape.

Weaving

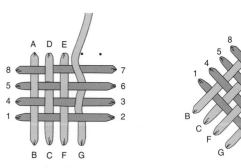
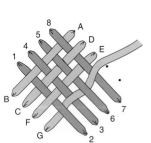

This technique can be used to fill any space. Follow numerical sequence to work horizontal Straight Stitches (page 11) for the foundation.

Bring a new ribbon up at A and weave over and under the previously worked stitches, making sure ribbon does not twist; stitch down at B. Weave additional rows in alternating patterns. Continue to fill space in this manner. The foundation can also be laid with diagonal stitches weaving on the opposite diagonal.

Wrapped Bar

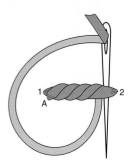

Make a Straight Stitch (page 11) of desired length (1-2). Then bring needle up at A, close to 1. Wrap the bar by slipping needle consecutively several times under the stitch; wrap to completely fill Straight Stitch. Stitch down to end.

Stitching Guides

The Stitching Guides for these designs are given in alphabetical order on the following pages. The front and back cover and color pages (17-20) show a full size stitched example of each design in the book. There is a key on the inside front cover so you can locate the guides for the front cover designs. The color pages and back cover examples include each design name and the page on which its guide is found.

The full size guides show the ribbon color and size to use in addition to the stitches required for the design. Refer to the Ribbon Color Conversion Key on page 61 for color suggestions using YLI or Bucilla brands of ribbon.

Six-strand cotton embroidery floss is sometimes used for stems, knots, or small design details. Unless otherwise directed, use two strands of floss. For stems, leaves, and tendrils, refer to the generic color name listed and select a floss color value similar to the same ribbon name. For other design details, choose a value that complements the design.

A Rose is a Rose
(see photo, back cover)

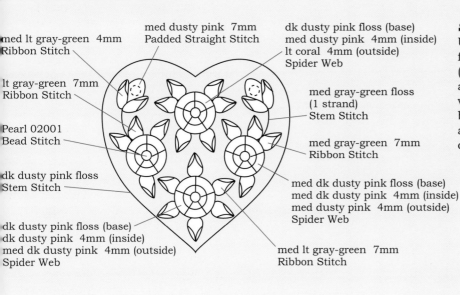

med lt gray-green 4mm
Ribbon Stitch

med dusty pink 7mm
Padded Straight Stitch

dk dusty pink floss (base)
med dusty pink 4mm (inside)
lt coral 4mm (outside)
Spider Web

lt gray-green 7mm
Ribbon Stitch

med gray-green floss
(1 strand)
Stem Stitch

Pearl 02001
Bead Stitch

med gray-green 7mm
Ribbon Stitch

dk dusty pink floss
Stem Stitch

med dk dusty pink floss (base)
med dk dusty pink 4mm (inside)
med dusty pink 4mm (outside)
Spider Web

dk dusty pink floss (base)
dk dusty pink 4mm (inside)
med dk dusty pink 4mm (outside)
Spider Web

med lt gray-green 7mm
Ribbon Stitch

Stitching order:
Use floss to Stem Stitch outline then work flower stems. Work Padded Straight Stitch (Straight Stitch over Straight Stitch) buds and Ribbon Stitch leaves. Use two color values for Spider Web roses; weave around base with darker value and finish outer area with lighter value. Attach a bead at center of each rose.

Acorn Wreath
(see photo, back cover)

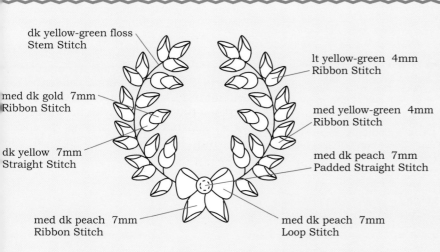

dk yellow-green floss
Stem Stitch

lt yellow-green 4mm
Ribbon Stitch

med dk gold 7mm
Ribbon Stitch

med yellow-green 4mm
Ribbon Stitch

dk yellow 7mm
Straight Stitch

med dk peach 7mm
Padded Straight Stitch

med dk peach 7mm
Ribbon Stitch

med dk peach 7mm
Loop Stitch

Stitching order:
Use floss to work curved Stem Stitch outlines. Work Ribbon Stitch leaves. For each bud, work a Ribbon Stitch on top of a Straight Stitch. For bow, work two Ribbon Stitches, two Loop Stitches, and a Padded Straight Stitch (Straight Stitch over French Knot).

Basket of Roses I

(see photo, page 18)

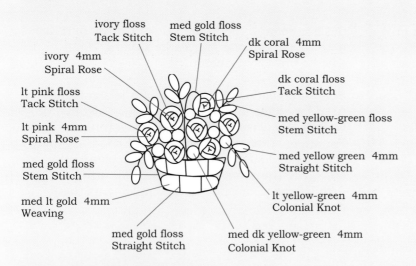

ivory floss
Tack Stitch

med gold floss
Stem Stitch

dk coral 4mm
Spiral Rose

ivory 4mm
Spiral Rose

dk coral floss
Tack Stitch

lt pink floss
Tack Stitch

med yellow-green floss
Stem Stitch

lt pink 4mm
Spiral Rose

med gold floss
Stem Stitch

med yellow green 4mm
Straight Stitch

med lt gold 4mm
Weaving

lt yellow-green 4mm
Colonial Knot

med gold floss
Straight Stitch

med dk yellow-green 4mm
Colonial Knot

Stitching order:

For basket, weave ribbon through floss Straight Stitches. Use floss to Stem Stitch basket outline, handle, and stems. Work Straight Stitch leaves. Work Spiral Roses in desired colors; tack with matching floss. Fill in spaces with Colonial Knots.

Basket of Roses II

(see photo, page 18)

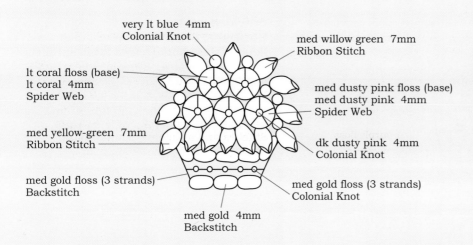

very lt blue 4mm
Colonial Knot

med willow green 7mm
Ribbon Stitch

lt coral floss (base)
lt coral 4mm
Spider Web

med dusty pink floss (base)
med dusty pink 4mm
Spider Web

med yellow-green 7mm
Ribbon Stitch

dk dusty pink 4mm
Colonial Knot

med gold floss (3 strands)
Backstitch

med gold floss (3 strands)
Colonial Knot

med gold 4mm
Backstitch

Stitching order:

Use ribbon to Backstitch top and bottom of basket. Use floss to Backstitch sides and front, adding Colonial Knots between Backstitches. Work Ribbon Stitch leaves and Spider Web roses with Colonial Knots at centers. Fill in spaces with Colonial Knots.

Bee & Flowers

(see photo, front cover)

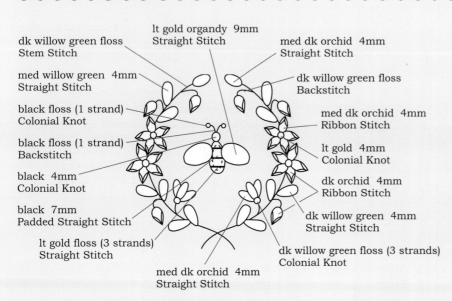

dk willow green floss
Stem Stitch

lt gold organdy 9mm
Straight Stitch

med dk orchid 4mm
Straight Stitch

med willow green 4mm
Straight Stitch

dk willow green floss
Backstitch

black floss (1 strand)
Colonial Knot

med dk orchid 4mm
Ribbon Stitch

black floss (1 strand)
Backstitch

lt gold 4mm
Colonial Knot

black 4mm
Colonial Knot

dk orchid 4mm
Ribbon Stitch

black 7mm
Padded Straight Stitch

dk willow green 4mm
Straight Stitch

lt gold floss (3 strands)
Straight Stitch

dk willow green floss (3 strands)
Colonial Knot

med dk orchid 4mm
Straight Stitch

Stitching order:

Use floss to work curved Stem Stitch main stems with Backstitch secondary stems. Work Straight Stitch leaves and partial flowers, adding floss Colonial Knots at each base. Work Ribbon Stitch buds and flowers with Colonial Knots at flower centers. For the bee, work a Padded Straight Stitch (Straight Stitch over Straight Stitch) topped with floss Straight Stitches. Work organdy Straight Stitches for wings. Work a Colonial Knot head. Use floss to work Backstitch with Colonial Knot antennae.

Beet Border

(see photo, page 20)

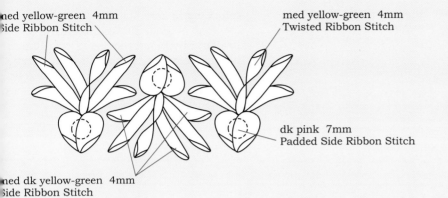

med yellow-green 4mm
Side Ribbon Stitch

med yellow-green 4mm
Twisted Ribbon Stitch

dk pink 7mm
Padded Side Ribbon Stitch

med dk yellow-green 4mm
Side Ribbon Stitch

Stitching order:
Work Padded Side Ribbon Stitch (two Side
Ribbon Stitches over one Colonial Knot)
for each beet. Work leaves with Side
Ribbon Stitch or Twisted Ribbon Stitch.

Note: This design can be repeated to form
a continuous border.

Berries & Bud

(see photo, page 17)

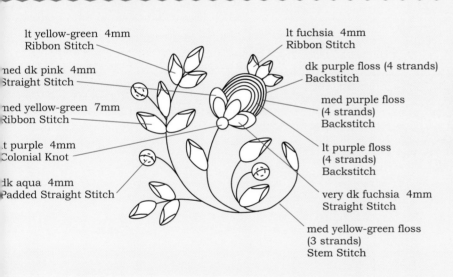

lt yellow-green 4mm
Ribbon Stitch

med dk pink 4mm
Straight Stitch

med yellow-green 7mm
Ribbon Stitch

lt purple 4mm
Colonial Knot

dk aqua 4mm
Padded Straight Stitch

lt fuchsia 4mm
Ribbon Stitch

dk purple floss (4 strands)
Backstitch

med purple floss
(4 strands)
Backstitch

lt purple floss
(4 strands)
Backstitch

very dk fuchsia 4mm
Straight Stitch

med yellow-green floss
(3 strands)
Stem Stitch

Stitching order:
Use floss to Stem Stitch stems. Add
Ribbon Stitch leaves. Work Padded
Straight Stitch (two Straight Stitches over
one Colonial Knot) buds. For main flower,
use three color values of floss to work
curving rows of Backstitch. Add three
Straight Stitches topped with Straight
Stitches and a Colonial Knot at base.
Work three Ribbon Stitches at top.

Berry Border

(see photo, back cover)

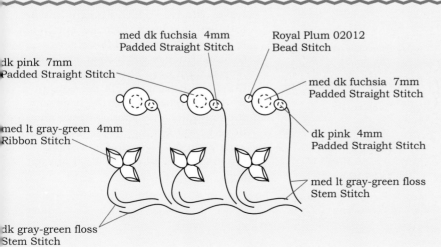

med dk fuchsia 4mm
Padded Straight Stitch

Royal Plum 02012
Bead Stitch

dk pink 7mm
Padded Straight Stitch

med dk fuchsia 7mm
Padded Straight Stitch

dk pink 4mm
Padded Straight Stitch

med lt gray-green 4mm
Ribbon Stitch

med lt gray-green floss
Stem Stitch

dk gray-green floss
Stem Stitch

Stitching order:
Use floss to Stem Stitch stems and border
lines. Work Ribbon Stitch leaves loosely.
For each berry, alternate color values and
work Padded Straight Stitch (Straight
Stitch over Colonial Knot) with a Padded
Straight Stitch (Straight Stitch over
Colonial Knot) at base; attach a bead at
top.

Note: This design can be repeated to form
a continuous border.

Berry Sprig

(see photo, back cover)

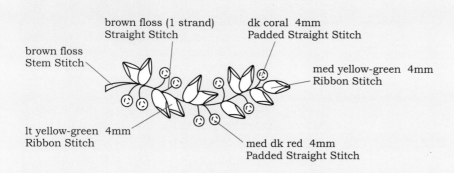

brown floss (1 strand)
Straight Stitch

dk coral 4mm
Padded Straight Stitch

brown floss
Stem Stitch

med yellow-green 4mm
Ribbon Stitch

lt yellow-green 4mm
Ribbon Stitch

med dk red 4mm
Padded Straight Stitch

Stitching order:
Use floss to Stem Stitch branch and Straight Stitch berry stems. Work Ribbon Stitch leaves and Padded Straight Stitch (Straight Stitch over French Knot) berries.

Berry Square

(see photo, front cover)

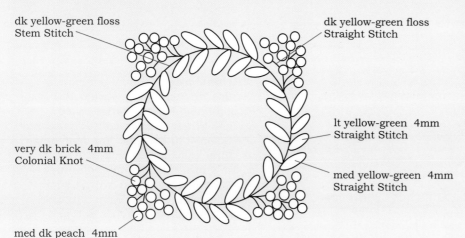

dk yellow-green floss
Stem Stitch

dk yellow-green floss
Straight Stitch

lt yellow-green 4mm
Straight Stitch

very dk brick 4mm
Colonial Knot

med yellow-green 4mm
Straight Stitch

med dk peach 4mm
Colonial Knot

Stitching order:
Use floss to Stem Stitch circular stem and Straight Stitch berry stems. Work Straight Stitch leaves and Colonial Knot berries.

Butterfly & Blossoms

(see photo, page 19)

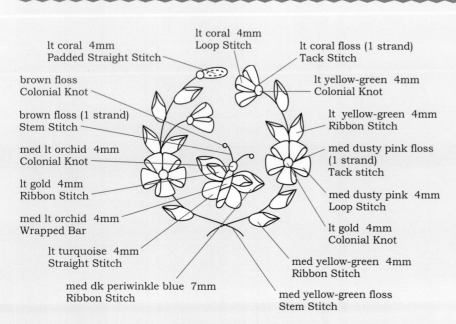

lt coral 4mm
Padded Straight Stitch

lt coral 4mm
Loop Stitch

lt coral floss (1 strand)
Tack Stitch

brown floss
Colonial Knot

lt yellow-green 4mm
Colonial Knot

brown floss (1 strand)
Stem Stitch

lt yellow-green 4mm
Ribbon Stitch

med lt orchid 4mm
Colonial Knot

med dusty pink floss
(1 strand)
Tack stitch

lt gold 4mm
Ribbon Stitch

med dusty pink 4mm
Loop Stitch

med lt orchid 4mm
Wrapped Bar

lt gold 4mm
Colonial Knot

lt turquoise 4mm
Straight Stitch

med yellow-green 4mm
Ribbon Stitch

med dk periwinkle blue 7mm
Ribbon Stitch

med yellow-green floss
Stem Stitch

Stitching order:
Use floss to work curved Stem Stitch branches and a stem. Work Ribbon Stitch leaves. Work a Padded Straight Stitch (Straight Stitch over Straight Stitch) bud and Loop Stitch partial flowers with Colonial Knots at each base. For each full flower, work Loop Stitch petals and a Colonial Knot center. For the butterfly, work a Wrapped Bar for the body with Ribbon Stitch over Ribbon Stitch and Straight Stitch wings. Work a Colonial Knot head. Use floss to Stem Stitch antennae; add a Colonial Knot at each end.

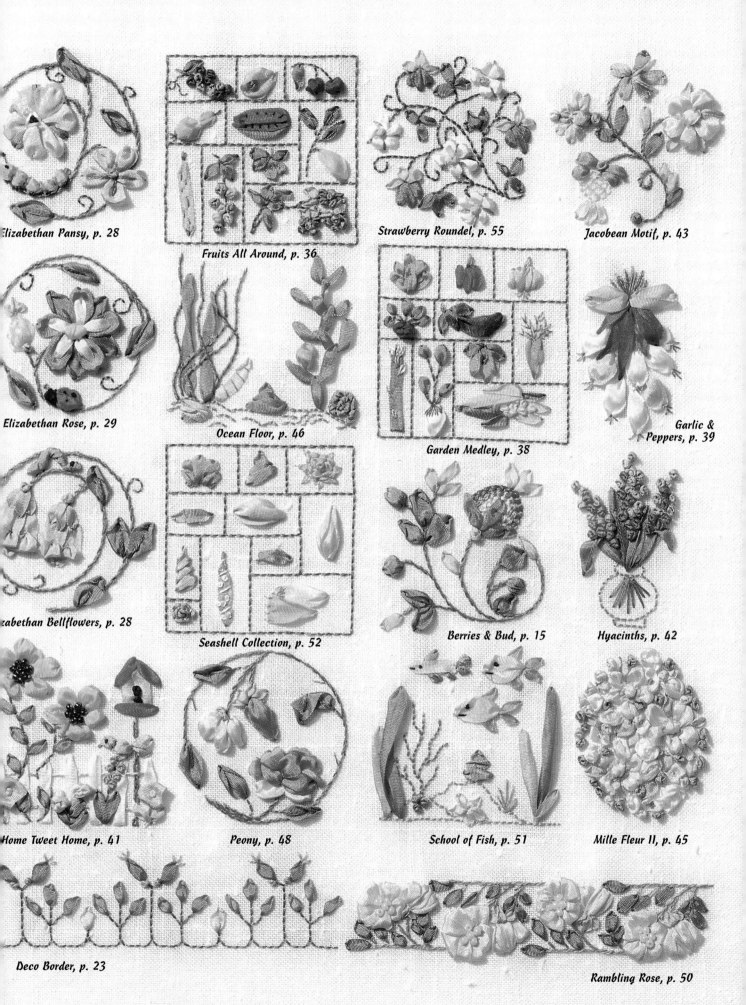

Elizabethan Pansy, p. 28

Fruits All Around, p. 36

Strawberry Roundel, p. 55

Jacobean Motif, p. 43

Elizabethan Rose, p. 29

Ocean Floor, p. 46

Garden Medley, p. 38

Garlic & Peppers, p. 39

Elizabethan Bellflowers, p. 28

Seashell Collection, p. 52

Berries & Bud, p. 15

Hyacinths, p. 42

Home Tweet Home, p. 41

Peony, p. 48

School of Fish, p. 51

Mille Fleur II, p. 45

Deco Border, p. 23

Rambling Rose, p. 50

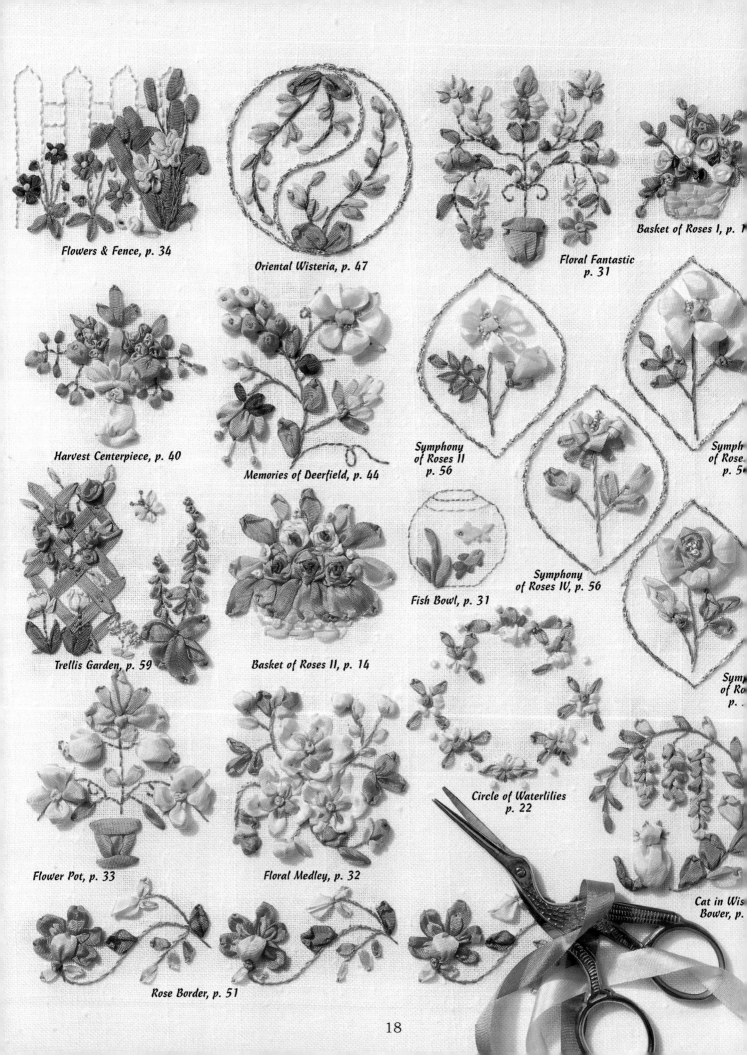

Flowers & Fence, p. 34

Oriental Wisteria, p. 47

Floral Fantastic
p. 31

Basket of Roses I, p. 1

Harvest Centerpiece, p. 40

Memories of Deerfield, p. 44

Symphony
of Roses II
p. 56

Symph
of Rose
p. 5

Trellis Garden, p. 59

Basket of Roses II, p. 14

Fish Bowl, p. 31

Symphony
of Roses IV, p. 56

Sym
of Ro
p.

Flower Pot, p. 33

Floral Medley, p. 32

Circle of Waterlilies
p. 22

Cat in Wis
Bower, p.

Rose Border, p. 51

Dutch Tile II, p. 26

Pansy Wreath, p. 47

Dutch Tile III, p. 26

Fruit Bowl, p. 35

Jacobean Tree, p. 43

Dutch Tile IV, p. 27

Dragonfly & Mum, p. 25

Full Load, p. 37

Knot Garden, p. 44

Country Shelf, p. 23

Butterfly & Blossoms, p. 16

Floral Parade, p. 32

Forget-Me-Nots, p. 34

Secret Place I, p. 52

Tree of Life, p.58

Thistles, p. 58

Violet Border, p. 59

19

Sewing Whatnots, p. 53

Country Bouquet, p. 22

Christmas Collection, p. 21

Christmas Swag, p. 22

Sunflower Sampling, p. 55

Gardening Whatnots, p. 39

Fruit Basket, p. 35

TULIP

Tulip Family Portrait, p. 59

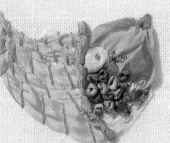

Harvest Cornucopia, p. 41

Easter Collection, p. 27

Della Robbia Tree, p. 24

Roly-Poly Santa, p. 50

Pumpkin Patch, p. 49

Halloween Whatnots, p. 40

Witch & Friends, p. 60

Pumpkin Basket, p. 49

Beet Border, p. 15

20

Cat in Wisteria Bower

(see photo, page 18)

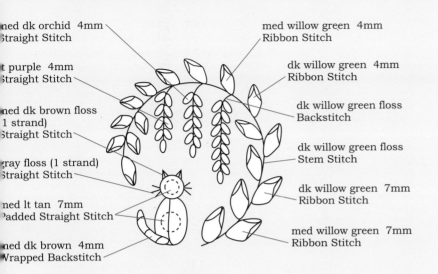

med dk orchid 4mm
Straight Stitch

lt purple 4mm
Straight Stitch

med dk brown floss
(1 strand)
Straight Stitch

gray floss (1 strand)
Straight Stitch

med lt tan 7mm
Padded Straight Stitch

med dk brown 4mm
Wrapped Backstitch

med willow green 4mm
Ribbon Stitch

dk willow green 4mm
Ribbon Stitch

dk willow green floss
Backstitch

dk willow green floss
Stem Stitch

dk willow green 7mm
Ribbon Stitch

med willow green 7mm
Ribbon Stitch

Stitching order:

Use floss Stem Stitch curved branch and Backstitch blossom stems. Work Ribbon Stitch leaves and Straight Stitch blossoms. For the cat, work Padded Straight Stitch (Straight Stitch over Colonial Knot) for body and head and Wrapped Backstitch for tail; use floss to Straight Stitch ears and whiskers.

Christmas Collection

(see photo, page 20)

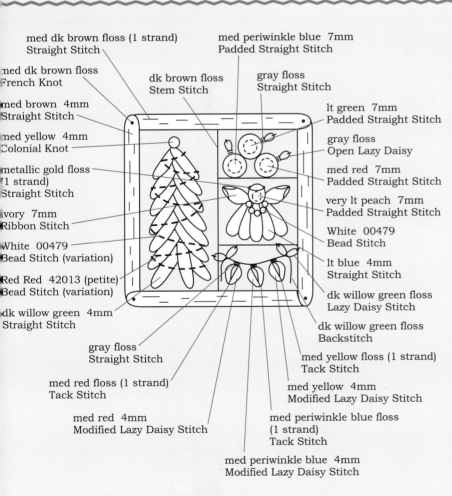

med dk brown floss (1 strand)
Straight Stitch

med dk brown floss
French Knot

med brown 4mm
Straight Stitch

med yellow 4mm
Colonial Knot

metallic gold floss
(1 strand)
Straight Stitch

ivory 7mm
Ribbon Stitch

White 00479
Bead Stitch (variation)

Red Red 42013 (petite)
Bead Stitch (variation)

dk willow green 4mm
Straight Stitch

gray floss
Straight Stitch

med red floss (1 strand)
Tack Stitch

med red 4mm
Modified Lazy Daisy Stitch

dk brown floss
Stem Stitch

med periwinkle blue 7mm
Padded Straight Stitch

gray floss
Straight Stitch

lt green 7mm
Padded Straight Stitch

gray floss
Open Lazy Daisy

med red 7mm
Padded Straight Stitch

very lt peach 7mm
Padded Straight Stitch

White 00479
Bead Stitch

lt blue 4mm
Straight Stitch

dk willow green floss
Lazy Daisy Stitch

dk willow green floss
Backstitch

med yellow floss (1 strand)
Tack Stitch

med yellow 4mm
Modified Lazy Daisy Stitch

med periwinkle blue floss
(1 strand)
Tack Stitch

med periwinkle blue 4mm
Modified Lazy Daisy Stitch

Stitching order:

Use floss to Stem Stitch separating outlines. For the tree, begin at the bottom and work Straight Stitches with ends overlapping toward middle. Work a loose Colonial Knot at top. Bring floss to front at top of tree. String beads, alternating three red and one white to fit top swag and secure floss at back; bring floss to front again. Continue to crisscross (shown by dashed line) tree and construct swag in same manner.

For each ornament, work a Padded Straight Stitch (Straight Stitch over Colonial Knot). Use floss to work an Open Lazy Daisy with Straight Stitches at base for each hanger.

For the angel, work Straight Stitches for dress, a Padded Straight Stitch (Straight Stitch over Colonial Knot) for head, and Ribbon Stitches for wings. Work a loose metallic floss Straight Stitch for halo. Attach seed beads arranged as a necklace.

For the string of lights, use floss to work Lazy Daisies and Backstitch string. For each light, work a Modified Lazy Daisy and use floss to Straight Stitch base.

For the frame, work long Straight Stitches; use floss to anchor each side with random Straight Stitches, adding a French Knot at each corner.

Christmas Swag

(see photo, page 20)

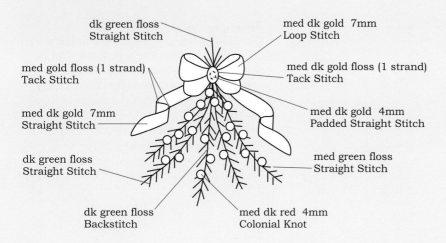

dk green floss
Straight Stitch

med dk gold 7mm
Loop Stitch

med gold floss (1 strand)
Tack Stitch

med dk gold floss (1 strand)
Tack Stitch

med dk gold 7mm
Straight Stitch

med dk gold 4mm
Padded Straight Stitch

dk green floss
Straight Stitch

med green floss
Straight Stitch

dk green floss
Backstitch

med dk red 4mm
Colonial Knot

Stitching order:
Use floss to Backstitch branches and Straight Stitch needles in a random color arrangement. Work Straight Stitch branch ends. Work Colonial Knot berries. For bow, tack Straight Stitch streamers in desired positions; work four Loop Stitches at top with a Padded Straight Stitch (Straight Stitch over Straight Stitch) at center.

Circle of Waterlilies

(see photo, page 18)

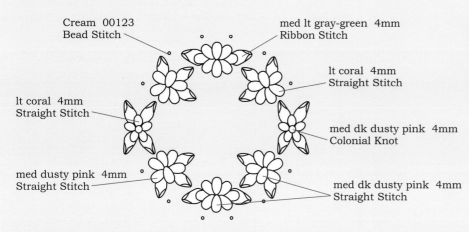

Cream 00123
Bead Stitch

med lt gray-green 4mm
Ribbon Stitch

lt coral 4mm
Straight Stitch

lt coral 4mm
Straight Stitch

med dk dusty pink 4mm
Colonial Knot

med dusty pink 4mm
Straight Stitch

med dk dusty pink 4mm
Straight Stitch

Stitching order:
Work Straight Stitch flowers. Work Ribbon Stitch leaves. Add a Colonial Knot at center of each open flower. Attach beads between flowers.

Country Bouquet

(see photo, page 20)

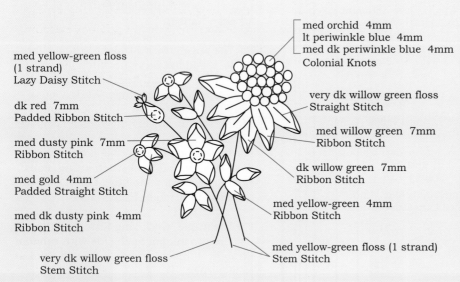

med yellow-green floss
(1 strand)
Lazy Daisy Stitch

med orchid 4mm
lt periwinkle blue 4mm
med dk periwinkle blue 4mm
Colonial Knots

dk red 7mm
Padded Ribbon Stitch

very dk willow green floss
Straight Stitch

med dusty pink 7mm
Ribbon Stitch

med willow green 7mm
Ribbon Stitch

med gold 4mm
Padded Straight Stitch

dk willow green 7mm
Ribbon Stitch

med dk dusty pink 4mm
Ribbon Stitch

med yellow-green 4mm
Ribbon Stitch

very dk willow green floss
Stem Stitch

med yellow-green floss (1 strand)
Stem Stitch

Stitching order:
Use floss to Stem Stitch stems. Work small Ribbon Stitch leaves. Work large Ribbon Stitch leaves with floss Straight Stitches centered on top for midribs.

For bud, work Padded Ribbon Stitch (Ribbon Stitch over Colonial Knot); use floss to work three Lazy Daisies at tip. For partial and full flowers, work Ribbon Stitch petals with a Padded Straight Stitch (Straight Stitch over Colonial Knot) for each center; on the full flower, make the stitches loosely. For large flower head, work Colonial Knots in a random color arrangement.

Country Shelf

(see photo, page 19)

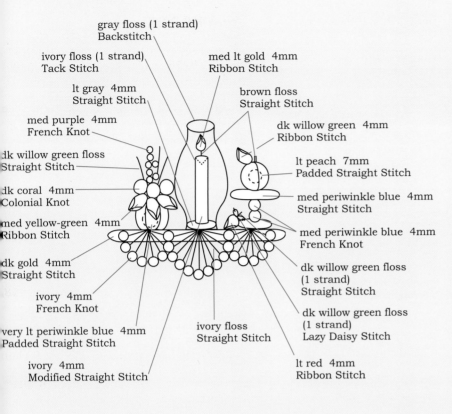

gray floss (1 strand)
Backstitch

ivory floss (1 strand)
Tack Stitch

lt gray 4mm
Straight Stitch

med purple 4mm
French Knot

dk willow green floss
Straight Stitch

dk coral 4mm
Colonial Knot

med yellow-green 4mm
Ribbon Stitch

dk gold 4mm
Straight Stitch

ivory 4mm
French Knot

very lt periwinkle blue 4mm
Padded Straight Stitch

ivory 4mm
Modified Straight Stitch

med lt gold 4mm
Ribbon Stitch

brown floss
Straight Stitch

dk willow green 4mm
Ribbon Stitch

lt peach 7mm
Padded Straight Stitch

med periwinkle blue 4mm
Straight Stitch

med periwinkle blue 4mm
French Knot

dk willow green floss
(1 strand)
Straight Stitch

dk willow green floss
(1 strand)
Lazy Daisy Stitch

ivory floss
Straight Stitch

lt red 4mm
Ribbon Stitch

Stitching order:

Use floss to Backstitch outline of globe. Work a Straight Stitch for base of globe and Modified Straight Stitch for candle, tacking it in place; add a Straight Stitch wick and Ribbon Stitch flame.

For the bouquet, work three Padded Straight Stitches (Straight Stitch over Colonial Knot) for vase. Work Ribbon Stitch leaves, Colonial Knot flowers, and a French Knot flower stalk. Use floss to Straight Stitch greenery.

For the fruit plate, work Straight Stitch base and top with French Knot pedestal. Work a Ribbon Stitch strawberry; use floss to top with a Straight Stitch stem and Lazy Daisy leaves. For the peach, work a Padded Straight Stitch (two Straight Stitches over one Colonial Knot) and a Ribbon Stitch leaf. Use floss to work a Straight Stitch stem.

Work a Straight Stitch for shelf. For the lace, work floss Straight Stitches and ribbon French Knots.

Deco Border

(see photo, page 17)

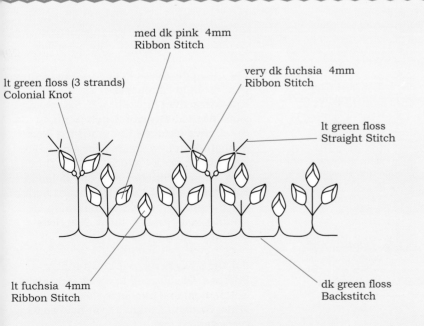

med dk pink 4mm
Ribbon Stitch

very dk fuchsia 4mm
Ribbon Stitch

lt green floss (3 strands)
Colonial Knot

lt green floss
Straight Stitch

lt fuchsia 4mm
Ribbon Stitch

dk green floss
Backstitch

Stitching order:

Use floss to Backstitch baseline and stems. Work loose Ribbon Stitches in three color values for buds; use floss to work a Colonial Knot at base of each dark value bud and Straight Stitches extending from tip.

Note: This design can be repeated to form a continuous border.

Delft Tile

(see photo, back cover)

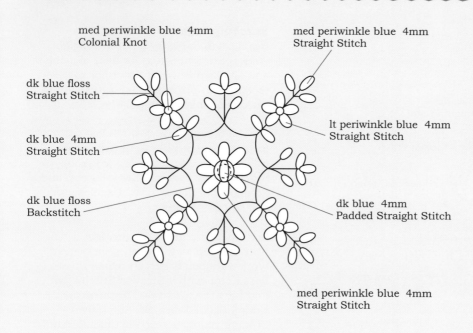

med periwinkle blue 4mm
Colonial Knot

med periwinkle blue 4mm
Straight Stitch

dk blue floss
Straight Stitch

lt periwinkle blue 4mm
Straight Stitch

dk blue 4mm
Straight Stitch

dk blue floss
Backstitch

dk blue 4mm
Padded Straight Stitch

med periwinkle blue 4mm
Straight Stitch

Stitching order:
Use floss to Backstitch central outline and Straight Stitch the stems. For the central flower, work Straight Stitch petals with a Padded Straight Stitch (three Straight Stitches over one Colonial Knot) at center. Work remaining Straight Stitch petals and leaves, adding a Colonial Knot at center of each full flower.

Della Robia Tree

(see photo, page 20)

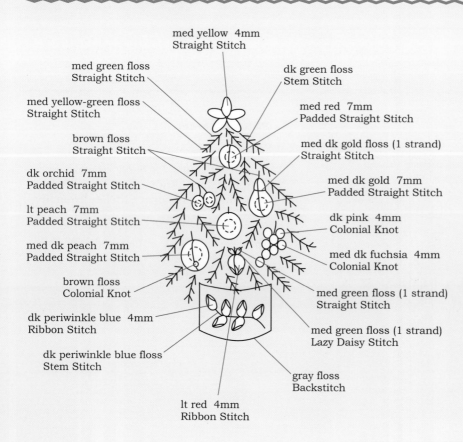

med yellow 4mm
Straight Stitch

med green floss
Straight Stitch

dk green floss
Stem Stitch

med yellow-green floss
Straight Stitch

med red 7mm
Padded Straight Stitch

brown floss
Straight Stitch

med dk gold floss (1 strand)
Straight Stitch

dk orchid 7mm
Padded Straight Stitch

med dk gold 7mm
Padded Straight Stitch

lt peach 7mm
Padded Straight Stitch

dk pink 4mm
Colonial Knot

med dk peach 7mm
Padded Straight Stitch

med dk fuchsia 4mm
Colonial Knot

brown floss
Colonial Knot

med green floss (1 strand)
Straight Stitch

dk periwinkle blue 4mm
Ribbon Stitch

med green floss (1 strand)
Lazy Daisy Stitch

dk periwinkle blue floss
Stem Stitch

gray floss
Backstitch

lt red 4mm
Ribbon Stitch

Stitching order:
For tree holder, use floss to Backstitch outline and Stem Stitch stem. Work Ribbon Stitch leaves.

For tree, use floss to Stem Stitch main stems; use a random arrangement of two color values to Straight Stitch needles.

For the apple, work Padded Straight Stitch (two Straight Stitches over one Colonial Knot). For the plums, peach, and pear, work Padded Straight Stitch (Straight Stitch over Colonial Knot); work a floss Straight Stitch to create pear shape. For the orange, work Padded Straight Stitch (two Straight Stitches over one Colonial Knot); add a floss Colonial Knot at bottom. For the grapes, work Colonial Knots in a random color arrangement. Add floss Straight Stitch stems.

For the strawberry, work two Ribbon Stitches. Use floss to top with a Straight Stitch stem and two Lazy Daisy leaves. Add a Straight Stitch star at top, working center stitch last.

Dragonfly & Mum

(see photo, page 19)

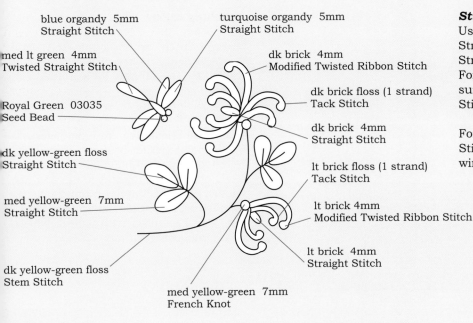

blue organdy 5mm
Straight Stitch

turquoise organdy 5mm
Straight Stitch

med lt green 4mm
Twisted Straight Stitch

dk brick 4mm
Modified Twisted Ribbon Stitch

Royal Green 03035
Seed Bead

dk brick floss (1 strand)
Tack Stitch

dk yellow-green floss
Straight Stitch

dk brick 4mm
Straight Stitch

med yellow-green 7mm
Straight Stitch

lt brick floss (1 strand)
Tack Stitch

lt brick 4mm
Modified Twisted Ribbon Stitch

dk yellow-green floss
Stem Stitch

lt brick 4mm
Straight Stitch

med yellow-green 7mm
French Knot

Stitching order:

Use floss to Stem Stitch stems. Work Straight Stitch leaves; use floss to add a Straight Stitch midrib centered on each. For each flower, work one Straight Stitch surrounded by Modified Twisted Ribbon Stitches; add a French Knot at base.

For the dragonfly, work a Twisted Straight Stitch body; add organdy Straight Stitch wings. Attach two beads for eyes.

Dutch Tile 1

(see photo, front cover)

med periwinkle blue 4mm
Padded Straight Stitch

dk brick 4mm
Straight Stitch

dk blue floss
Backstitch

med yellow 4mm
Colonial Knot

dk blue floss
Colonial Knot

dk yellow-green floss
Straight Stitch

dk blue 4mm
Padded Straight
Stitch

dk yellow-green floss
Backstitch

dk blue floss
Stem Stitch

lt peach 4mm
Padded Straight Stitch

med dk peach 7mm
Padded Straight Stitch

dk yellow-green floss
Stem Stitch

med yellow-green 4mm
Ribbon Stitch

dk yellow 4mm
Straight Stitch

Stitching order:

Use floss to Stem Stitch outlines and Backstitch corner motif lines; add Colonial Knots at ends of curliques. For each corner motif, work three Padded Straight Stitches (Straight Stitch over Colonial Knot).

For center flower, use floss to Stem Stitch, Straight Stitch, and Backstitch stems. Work Straight Stitches for base and Ribbon Stitches for leaves. For full flower, work Straight Stitch petals and a Colonial Knot at center. For buds, work Padded Straight Stitch (Straight Stitch over Colonial Knot).

Dutch Tile II

(see photo, page 19)

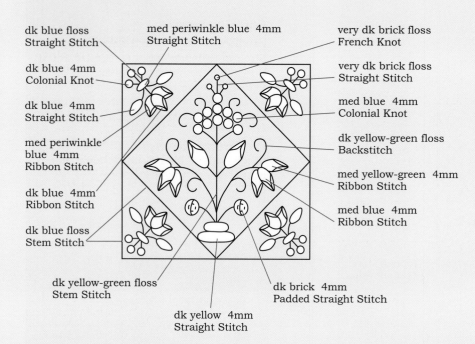

dk blue floss
Straight Stitch

med periwinkle blue 4mm
Straight Stitch

very dk brick floss
French Knot

dk blue 4mm
Colonial Knot

very dk brick floss
Straight Stitch

dk blue 4mm
Straight Stitch

med blue 4mm
Colonial Knot

med periwinkle
blue 4mm
Ribbon Stitch

dk yellow-green floss
Backstitch

dk blue 4mm
Ribbon Stitch

med yellow-green 4mm
Ribbon Stitch

dk blue floss
Stem Stitch

med blue 4mm
Ribbon Stitch

dk yellow-green floss
Stem Stitch

dk brick 4mm
Padded Straight Stitch

dk yellow 4mm
Straight Stitch

Stitching order:

Use floss to Stem Stitch outlines and Straight Stitch corner motif lines. Work three Straight Stitches, three Colonial Knots, and overlapping Ribbon Stitches for each corner motif.

For center flower, use floss to Stem Stitch stems and Backstitch curliques. Work Straight Stitches for base and Ribbon Stitch for leaves and buds. For berries, work loose Colonial Knots at top and two Padded Straight Stitches (two Straight Stitches over one Colonial Knot) at bottom. Use floss to work Straight Stitches and French Knots at top.

Dutch Tile III

(see photo, page 19)

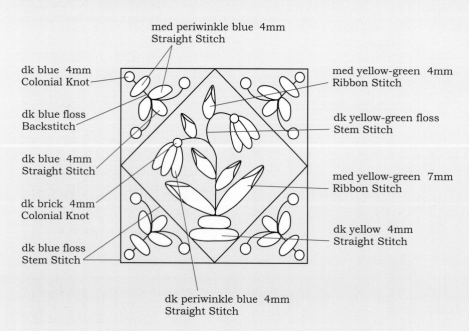

med periwinkle blue 4mm
Straight Stitch

dk blue 4mm
Colonial Knot

med yellow-green 4mm
Ribbon Stitch

dk blue floss
Backstitch

dk yellow-green floss
Stem Stitch

dk blue 4mm
Straight Stitch

med yellow-green 7mm
Ribbon Stitch

dk brick 4mm
Colonial Knot

dk yellow 4mm
Straight Stitch

dk blue floss
Stem Stitch

dk periwinkle blue 4mm
Straight Stitch

Stitching order:

Use floss to Stem Stitch outlines and Backstitch corner motif lines. For each corner motif, work four Straight Stitches and three Colonial Knots.

For center flower, use floss to Stem Stitch stems. Work Straight Stitches for base and Ribbon Stitch for leaves. For each blossom, work three overlapping Straight Stitches with a Colonial Knot at base.

Dutch Tile IV

(see photo, page 19)

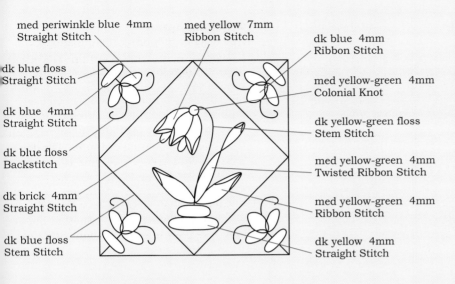

med periwinkle blue 4mm
Straight Stitch

med yellow 7mm
Ribbon Stitch

dk blue 4mm
Ribbon Stitch

med yellow-green 4mm
Colonial Knot

dk blue floss
Straight Stitch

dk yellow-green floss
Stem Stitch

dk blue 4mm
Straight Stitch

med yellow-green 4mm
Twisted Ribbon Stitch

dk blue floss
Backstitch

med yellow-green 4mm
Ribbon Stitch

dk brick 4mm
Straight Stitch

dk yellow 4mm
Straight Stitch

dk blue floss
Stem Stitch

Stitching order:

Use floss to Stem Stitch outlines, Backstitch curliques, and Straight Stitch corner stems. Work Straight Stitches and a Ribbon Stitch for each corner motif.

For center flower, use floss to Stem Stitch stem. Work Straight Stitches for base. Work Ribbon Stitch and Twisted Ribbon Stitch leaves. Work Ribbon Stitch flower petals, adding Straight Stitch stamens and a Colonial Knot at base.

Easter Collection

(see photo, page 20)

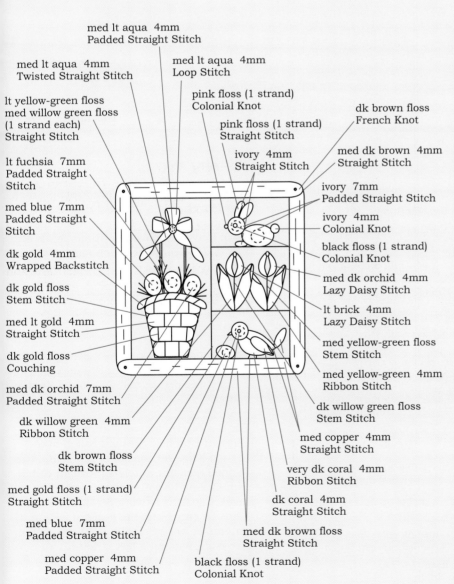

med lt aqua 4mm
Padded Straight Stitch

med lt aqua 4mm
Twisted Straight Stitch

med lt aqua 4mm
Loop Stitch

lt yellow-green floss
med willow green floss
(1 strand each)
Straight Stitch

pink floss (1 strand)
Colonial Knot

dk brown floss
French Knot

pink floss (1 strand)
Straight Stitch

med dk brown 4mm
Straight Stitch

lt fuchsia 7mm
Padded Straight
Stitch

ivory 4mm
Straight Stitch

med blue 7mm
Padded Straight
Stitch

ivory 7mm
Padded Straight Stitch

dk gold 4mm
Wrapped Backstitch

ivory 4mm
Colonial Knot

dk gold floss
Stem Stitch

black floss (1 strand)
Colonial Knot

med lt gold 4mm
Straight Stitch

med dk orchid 4mm
Lazy Daisy Stitch

lt brick 4mm
Lazy Daisy Stitch

dk gold floss
Couching

med yellow-green floss
Stem Stitch

med dk orchid 7mm
Padded Straight Stitch

med yellow-green 4mm
Ribbon Stitch

dk willow green 4mm
Ribbon Stitch

dk willow green floss
Stem Stitch

dk brown floss
Stem Stitch

med copper 4mm
Straight Stitch

med gold floss (1 strand)
Straight Stitch

very dk coral 4mm
Ribbon Stitch

med blue 7mm
Padded Straight Stitch

dk coral 4mm
Straight Stitch

med copper 4mm
Padded Straight Stitch

med dk brown floss
Straight Stitch

black floss (1 strand)
Colonial Knot

Stitching order:

Use floss to Stem Stitch separating outlines. Work Straight Stitches for basket, couched down with floss. Work Wrapped Backstitch for rim and use floss to Stem Stitch outline and handle. Work Padded Straight Stitch (Straight Stitch over Colonial Knot) for each egg. Use blended floss (one strand of each color) to Straight Stitch grass. For the bow, work Twisted Straight Stitch streamers, Loop Stitch loops, and a Padded Straight Stitch (Straight Stitch over Straight Stitch) for knot.

For the bunny, work a Padded Straight Stitch (Straight Stitch over Colonial Knot) for body and Padded Straight Stitch (Straight Stitch over French Knot) for head. Work Straight Stitches for ears and paw and a Colonial Knot for tail. Use floss to work a Straight Stitch along one ear and Colonial Knots for the nose and eye.

For the tulips, use floss to work Stem Stitch stems. Work Ribbon Stitch leaves and Lazy Daisy flowers.

For the bird section, work Straight Stitch breast, body, and tail, and a Ribbon Stitch wing. Add Padded Straight Stitch (Straight Stitch over Colonial Knot) for head and egg. Use floss to Straight Stitch beak and feet. Add a Colonial Knot eye.

For the frame, work long Straight Stitches; use floss to anchor each side with random Straight Stitches, adding a French Knot at each corner.

Elizabethan Bellflowers

(see photo, page 17)

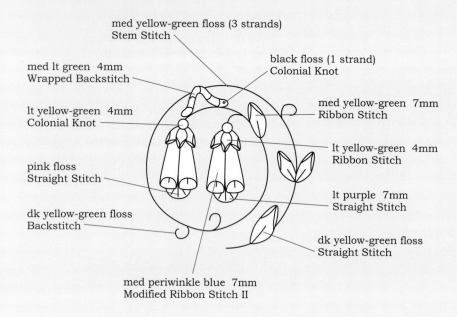

med yellow-green floss (3 strands)
Stem Stitch

med lt green 4mm
Wrapped Backstitch

lt yellow-green 4mm
Colonial Knot

pink floss
Straight Stitch

dk yellow-green floss
Backstitch

black floss (1 strand)
Colonial Knot

med yellow-green 7mm
Ribbon Stitch

lt yellow-green 4mm
Ribbon Stitch

lt purple 7mm
Straight Stitch

dk yellow-green floss
Straight Stitch

med periwinkle blue 7mm
Modified Ribbon Stitch II

Stitching order:

Use floss to Stem Stitch stem and Backstitch curliques. Work Ribbon Stitch leaves. Add a floss Straight Stitch for midrib of each leaf. For each flower, work one Straight Stitch covered by two overlapping Modified Ribbon Stitches II; use floss to add three Straight Stitches centered at bottom. At base of each flower work Ribbon Stitches for calyx plus a Colonial Knot.

For the worm, work Wrapped Backstitch and add a Colonial Knot eye.

Elizabethan Pansy

(see photo, page 17)

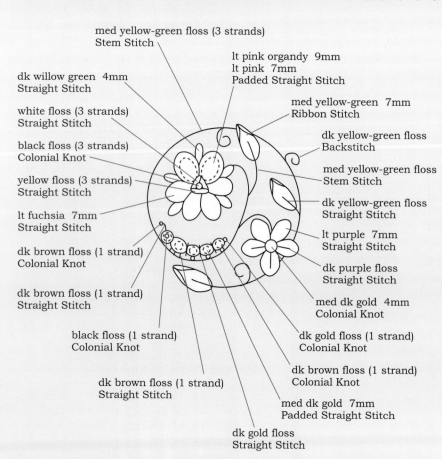

med yellow-green floss (3 strands)
Stem Stitch

dk willow green 4mm
Straight Stitch

white floss (3 strands)
Straight Stitch

black floss (3 strands)
Colonial Knot

yellow floss (3 strands)
Straight Stitch

lt fuchsia 7mm
Straight Stitch

dk brown floss (1 strand)
Colonial Knot

dk brown floss (1 strand)
Straight Stitch

black floss (1 strand)
Colonial Knot

dk brown floss (1 strand)
Straight Stitch

lt pink organdy 9mm
lt pink 7mm
Padded Straight Stitch

med yellow-green 7mm
Ribbon Stitch

dk yellow-green floss
Backstitch

med yellow-green floss
Stem Stitch

dk yellow-green floss
Straight Stitch

lt purple 7mm
Straight Stitch

dk purple floss
Straight Stitch

med dk gold 4mm
Colonial Knot

dk gold floss (1 strand)
Colonial Knot

dk brown floss (1 strand)
Colonial Knot

med dk gold 7mm
Padded Straight Stitch

dk gold floss
Straight Stitch

Stitching order:

Use floss to Stem Stitch stem and Backstitch curliques. Work Ribbon Stitch vine leaves. Add a floss Straight Stitch for midrib of each leaf. For the pink pansy, work four loose Straight Stitch petals and two Padded Straight Stitch (organdy Straight Stitch over silk Straight Stitch) petals; add Straight Stitches between petals. Use floss to work a Colonial Knot at center and loose Straight Stitches around knot.

For the purple pansy, work Straight Stitch petals with floss Straight Stitches on lower three petals; add a Colonial Knot at center.

For the caterpillar, work three Padded Straight Stitches (Straight Stitch over French Knot) for the small segments, two Padded Straight Stitches (Straight Stitch over Colonial Knot) for large segment and head. Use floss to work Straight Stitches between segments, the forward feet, and antennae; work Colonial Knot eye, antennae end, remaining feet, and tail.

28

Elizabethan Pea Pods

(see photo, front cover)

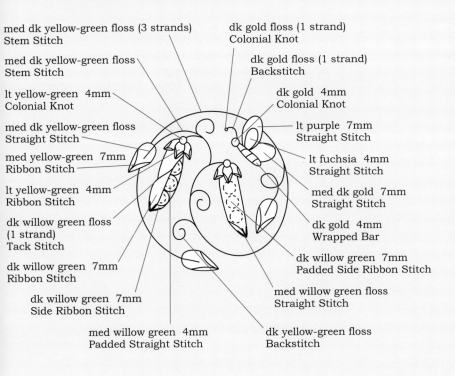

med dk yellow-green floss (3 strands)
Stem Stitch

med dk yellow-green floss
Stem Stitch

lt yellow-green 4mm
Colonial Knot

med dk yellow-green floss
Straight Stitch

med yellow-green 7mm
Ribbon Stitch

lt yellow-green 4mm
Ribbon Stitch

dk willow green floss
(1 strand)
Tack Stitch

dk willow green 7mm
Ribbon Stitch

dk willow green 7mm
Side Ribbon Stitch

med willow green 4mm
Padded Straight Stitch

dk gold floss (1 strand)
Colonial Knot

dk gold floss (1 strand)
Backstitch

dk gold 4mm
Colonial Knot

lt purple 7mm
Straight Stitch

lt fuchsia 4mm
Straight Stitch

med dk gold 7mm
Straight Stitch

dk gold 4mm
Wrapped Bar

dk willow green 7mm
Padded Side Ribbon Stitch

med willow green floss
Straight Stitch

dk yellow-green floss
Backstitch

Stitching order:
Use floss to Stem Stitch stems and Backstitch tendrils. Work Ribbon Stitch leaves. Add a floss Straight Stitch for midrib of each leaf.

For open pea pod, work a Side Ribbon Stitch topped with three Padded Straight Stitches (Straight Stitch over Colonial Knot). Cover knots with a loose Ribbon Stitch, tacked open to reveal partial row of peas. For closed pea pod, work a Padded Side Ribbon Stitch (one Side Ribbon Stitch over three Colonial Knots); tack edges in place. On each pea pod, use floss to Straight Stitch tip; at base add Ribbon Stitches for calyx plus a Colonial Knot.

For butterfly, work a Wrapped Bar body and a Colonial Knot head; use floss to Backstitch antennae, adding a Colonial Knot at tip. Add Straight Stitch wings, working one stitch over another for upper wing.

Elizabethan Rose

(see photo, page 17)

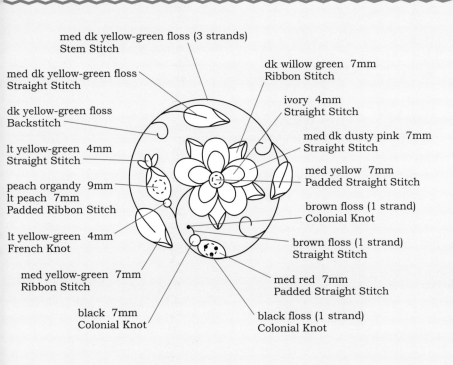

med dk yellow-green floss (3 strands)
Stem Stitch

med dk yellow-green floss
Straight Stitch

dk yellow-green floss
Backstitch

lt yellow-green 4mm
Straight Stitch

peach organdy 9mm
lt peach 7mm
Padded Ribbon Stitch

lt yellow-green 4mm
French Knot

med yellow-green 7mm
Ribbon Stitch

black 7mm
Colonial Knot

dk willow green 7mm
Ribbon Stitch

ivory 4mm
Straight Stitch

med dk dusty pink 7mm
Straight Stitch

med yellow 7mm
Padded Straight Stitch

brown floss (1 strand)
Colonial Knot

brown floss (1 strand)
Straight Stitch

med red 7mm
Padded Straight Stitch

black floss (1 strand)
Colonial Knot

Stitching order:
Use floss to Stem Stitch stems and Backstitch curliques. Work Ribbon Stitch leaves. Add a floss Straight Stitch for midrib of each leaf.

For the bud, work Padded Ribbon Stitch (Ribbon Stitch over Colonial Knot), then cover it with an organdy Ribbon Stitch. Add Straight Stitches at tip and a French Knot at base. For the full flower, work Ribbon Stitches for calyx. Add Straight Stitches on top of Straight Stitches for petals. Work a Padded Straight Stitch (Straight Stitch over Colonial Knot) at center.

For the ladybug, work a Padded Straight Stitch (Straight Stitch over Colonial Knot) body and a Colonial Knot head. Use floss to work Colonial Knot spots plus a Straight Stitch with a Colonial Knot for antenna.

English Border Garden

(see photo, front cover)

Stitching order:

Use floss to Stem Stitch or Straight Stitch all stems; or, if desired, complete each group of flowers before proceeding to the next.

Beginning with the back left sunflowers, work Ribbon Stitch leaves; work Straight Stitch petals surrounding floss Colonial Knot centers. For the blue columnar flowers, work three color values of French Knots with darkest values toward base of column. For back right flower, begin at the bottom and work Ribbon Stitches, Straight Stitches, Colonial Knots, and French Knots.

For the front left flowers, work Ribbon Stitch leaves with loose Colonial Knot flowers. For the center front group, work Straight Stitch leaves and Modified Loop Stitch flowers held down with a floss Colonial Knot at each center. For the front right group, work Straight Stitch leaves; work French Knot petals surrounding a floss Colonial Knot center.

For the bee, work a Ribbon Stitch topped with floss Straight Stitches. Work organdy Straight Stitches for wings. Work a floss Colonial Knot head.

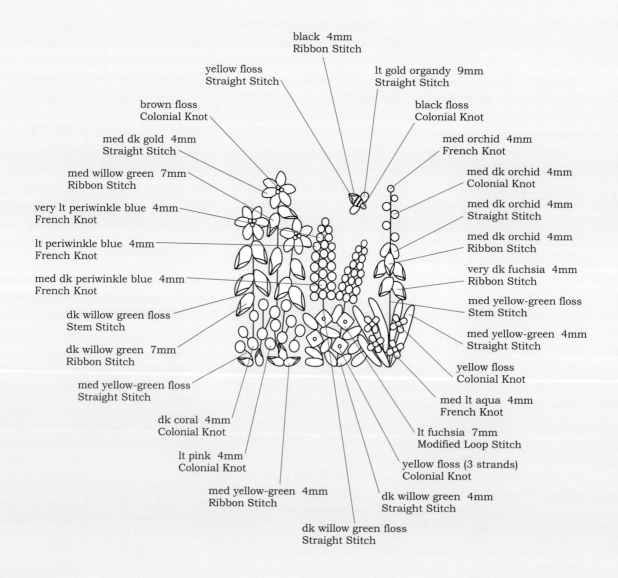

black 4mm
Ribbon Stitch

yellow floss
Straight Stitch

lt gold organdy 9mm
Straight Stitch

brown floss
Colonial Knot

black floss
Colonial Knot

med dk gold 4mm
Straight Stitch

med orchid 4mm
French Knot

med willow green 7mm
Ribbon Stitch

med dk orchid 4mm
Colonial Knot

very lt periwinkle blue 4mm
French Knot

med dk orchid 4mm
Straight Stitch

lt periwinkle blue 4mm
French Knot

med dk orchid 4mm
Ribbon Stitch

med dk periwinkle blue 4mm
French Knot

very dk fuchsia 4mm
Ribbon Stitch

med yellow-green floss
Stem Stitch

dk willow green floss
Stem Stitch

med yellow-green 4mm
Straight Stitch

dk willow green 7mm
Ribbon Stitch

yellow floss
Colonial Knot

med yellow-green floss
Straight Stitch

med lt aqua 4mm
French Knot

dk coral 4mm
Colonial Knot

lt fuchsia 7mm
Modified Loop Stitch

lt pink 4mm
Colonial Knot

yellow floss (3 strands)
Colonial Knot

med yellow-green 4mm
Ribbon Stitch

dk willow green 4mm
Straight Stitch

dk willow green floss
Straight Stitch

Fish Bowl

(see photo, page 18)

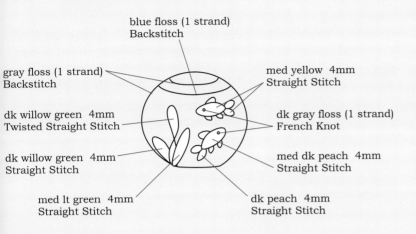

blue floss (1 strand)
Backstitch

gray floss (1 strand)
Backstitch

med yellow 4mm
Straight Stitch

dk willow green 4mm
Twisted Straight Stitch

dk gray floss (1 strand)
French Knot

dk willow green 4mm
Straight Stitch

med dk peach 4mm
Straight Stitch

med lt green 4mm
Straight Stitch

dk peach 4mm
Straight Stitch

Stitching order:
Use floss to Backstitch bowl outline and
water line. Work Straight Stitch and
Twisted Straight Stitch leaves. For each
fish, work Straight Stitches and add a
floss French Knot eye.

Floral Fantastic

(see photo, page 18)

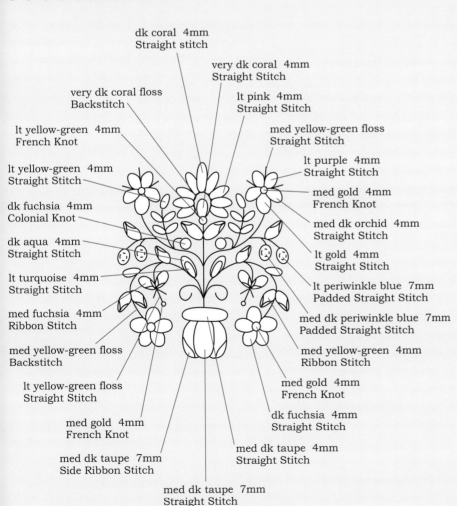

dk coral 4mm
Straight stitch

very dk coral 4mm
Straight Stitch

lt pink 4mm
Straight Stitch

very dk coral floss
Backstitch

med yellow-green floss
Straight Stitch

lt yellow-green 4mm
French Knot

lt purple 4mm
Straight Stitch

lt yellow-green 4mm
Straight Stitch

med gold 4mm
French Knot

dk fuchsia 4mm
Colonial Knot

med dk orchid 4mm
Straight Stitch

dk aqua 4mm
Straight Stitch

lt gold 4mm
Straight Stitch

lt turquoise 4mm
Straight Stitch

lt periwinkle blue 7mm
Padded Straight Stitch

med fuchsia 4mm
Ribbon Stitch

med dk periwinkle blue 7mm
Padded Straight Stitch

med yellow-green floss
Backstitch

med yellow-green 4mm
Ribbon Stitch

lt yellow-green floss
Straight Stitch

med gold 4mm
French Knot

med gold 4mm
French Knot

dk fuchsia 4mm
Straight Stitch

med dk taupe 7mm
Side Ribbon Stitch

med dk taupe 4mm
Straight Stitch

med dk taupe 7mm
Straight Stitch

Stitching order:
Use floss to Backstitch stems. Work
Straight Stitch and Ribbon Stitch leaves.

For center flower, work Straight Stitch
center and petals. Work a French Knot at
base and use floss to work oval outline.

For the purple flowers, work Straight
Stitch petals with a French Knot center;
add floss Straight Stitches between petals.

For the berries, work Colonial Knots and
Padded Straight Stitches (Straight Stitch
over French Knot). For the oval buds,
work small Straight Stitches on top of
larger Straight Stitches. For each partial
flower, work Ribbon Stitches. Use floss to
work Straight Stitches; then work a
French Knot at tip.

For each fuchsia flower, work Straight
Stitch petals with a French Knot center.
For flower pot, work Side Ribbon Stitches
and Straight Stitches.

Floral Medley

(see photo, page 18)

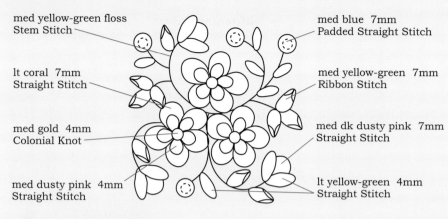

med yellow-green floss
Stem Stitch

lt coral 7mm
Straight Stitch

med gold 4mm
Colonial Knot

med dusty pink 4mm
Straight Stitch

med blue 7mm
Padded Straight Stitch

med yellow-green 7mm
Ribbon Stitch

med dk dusty pink 7mm
Straight Stitch

lt yellow-green 4mm
Straight Stitch

Stitching order:

Use floss to Stem Stitch stems. Work Straight Stitch and Ribbon Stitch leaves. For the berries, work Padded Straight Stitch (Straight Stitch over Colonial Knot).

Work a Straight Stitch for each bud; add two Straight Stitches for calyx. For each flower petal, work a Straight Stitch with a smaller Straight Stitch on top; add a Colonial Knot at center.

Floral Parade

(see photo, page 19)

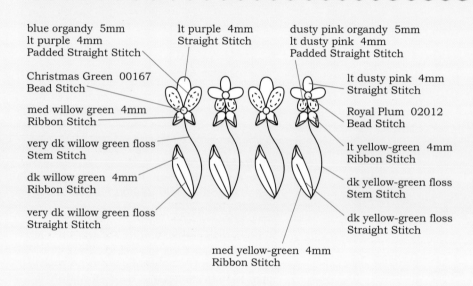

blue organdy 5mm
lt purple 4mm
Padded Straight Stitch

Christmas Green 00167
Bead Stitch

med willow green 4mm
Ribbon Stitch

very dk willow green floss
Stem Stitch

dk willow green 4mm
Ribbon Stitch

very dk willow green floss
Straight Stitch

lt purple 4mm
Straight Stitch

dusty pink organdy 5mm
lt dusty pink 4mm
Padded Straight Stitch

lt dusty pink 4mm
Straight Stitch

Royal Plum 02012
Bead Stitch

lt yellow-green 4mm
Ribbon Stitch

dk yellow-green floss
Stem Stitch

dk yellow-green floss
Straight Stitch

med yellow-green 4mm
Ribbon Stitch

Stitching order:

Use floss to Stem Stitch stems. Work Ribbon Stitch leaves; add a Straight Stitch midrib on each leaf. Work Ribbon Stitch calyxes.

For each purple flower, work a Straight Stitch for center petal and Padded Straight Stitch (organdy Straight Stitch over silk Straight Stitch) side petals; add a seed bead at base. For pink flowers, work three Straight Stitches for upper petals and Padded Straight Stitch (organdy Straight Stitch over silk Straight Stitch) for lower petals; add a seed bead at center.

Note: This design can be repeated to form a continuous border.

Floral Wreath

(see photo, back cover)

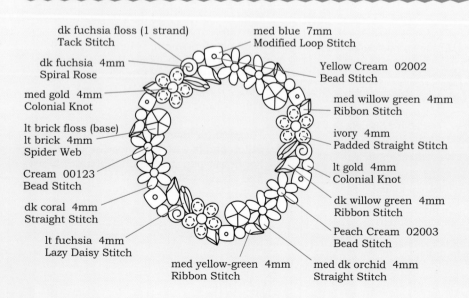

dk fuchsia floss (1 strand)
Tack Stitch

dk fuchsia 4mm
Spiral Rose

med gold 4mm
Colonial Knot

lt brick floss (base)
lt brick 4mm
Spider Web

Cream 00123
Bead Stitch

dk coral 4mm
Straight Stitch

lt fuchsia 4mm
Lazy Daisy Stitch

med yellow-green 4mm
Ribbon Stitch

med blue 7mm
Modified Loop Stitch

Yellow Cream 02002
Bead Stitch

med willow green 4mm
Ribbon Stitch

ivory 4mm
Padded Straight Stitch

lt gold 4mm
Colonial Knot

dk willow green 4mm
Ribbon Stitch

Peach Cream 02003
Bead Stitch

med dk orchid 4mm
Straight Stitch

Stitching order:

Work Ribbon Stitch leaves. Begin with ivory flower and proceed clockwise; this sequence appears three times around wreath. For ivory flower, work Padded Straight Stitch (Straight Stitch over French Knot) petals with a Colonial Knot center. For oval fuchsia bud, work a Lazy Daisy Stitch. For the three round flowers (fuchsia, gold, and blue), work a Spiral Rose, a loose Colonial Knot, and a Modified Loop Stitch with a bead at center.

For the coral and orchid flowers, work loose Straight Stitch petals with a bead at each center. For brick flower, work a Spider Web Rose. Fill in remaining space with a loose Colonial Knot and Modified Loop Stitch with a bead at center. Fill in with additional Ribbon Stitch leaves.

Flower Pot

(see photo, page 18)

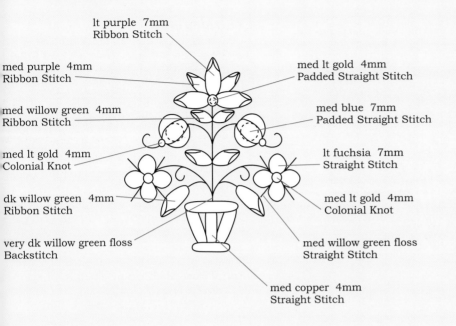

lt purple 7mm
Ribbon Stitch

med purple 4mm
Ribbon Stitch

med willow green 4mm
Ribbon Stitch

med lt gold 4mm
Colonial Knot

dk willow green 4mm
Ribbon Stitch

very dk willow green floss
Backstitch

med lt gold 4mm
Padded Straight Stitch

med blue 7mm
Padded Straight Stitch

lt fuchsia 7mm
Straight Stitch

med lt gold 4mm
Colonial Knot

med willow green floss
Straight Stitch

med copper 4mm
Straight Stitch

Stitching order:

Use floss to Backstitch stems and curliques. Work Ribbon Stitch leaves. For purple flower, work two Ribbon Stitch petals covered with three loose Ribbon Stitch petals. Work a Padded Straight Stitch (Straight Stitch over French Knot) at base.

For blue flowers, work Padded Straight Stitch (three Straight Stitches over one Colonial Knot); add a Colonial Knot at tip. For pink flowers, work loose Straight Stitch petals with a Colonial Knot at center. Use floss to work Straight Stitches between petals.

For flower pot, work Straight Stitches, overlapping for sides, then add top and bottom.

Flower Square

(see photo, front cover)

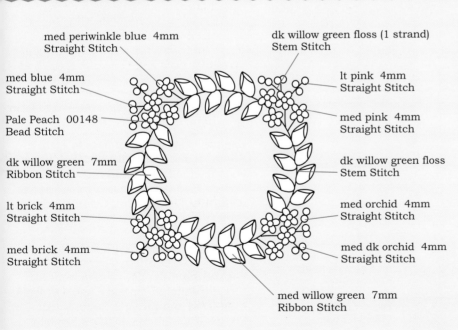

med periwinkle blue 4mm
Straight Stitch

med blue 4mm
Straight Stitch

Pale Peach 00148
Bead Stitch

dk willow green 7mm
Ribbon Stitch

lt brick 4mm
Straight Stitch

med brick 4mm
Straight Stitch

dk willow green floss (1 strand)
Stem Stitch

lt pink 4mm
Straight Stitch

med pink 4mm
Straight Stitch

dk willow green floss
Stem Stitch

med orchid 4mm
Straight Stitch

med dk orchid 4mm
Straight Stitch

med willow green 7mm
Ribbon Stitch

Stitching order:

Use floss to Stem Stitch stems. Work Ribbon Stitch leaves. For each group of flowers, work Straight Stitch petals in two color values. Attach a seed bead to each full flower center.

Flowers & Fence

(see photo, page 18)

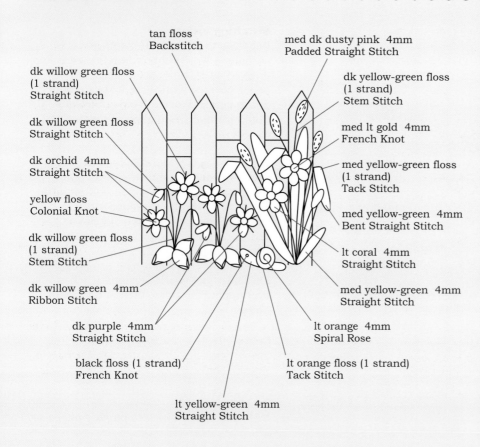

tan floss
Backstitch

med dk dusty pink 4mm
Padded Straight Stitch

dk willow green floss
(1 strand)
Straight Stitch

dk yellow-green floss
(1 strand)
Stem Stitch

dk willow green floss
Straight Stitch

med lt gold 4mm
French Knot

dk orchid 4mm
Straight Stitch

med yellow-green floss
(1 strand)
Tack Stitch

yellow floss
Colonial Knot

med yellow-green 4mm
Bent Straight Stitch

dk willow green floss
(1 strand)
Stem Stitch

lt coral 4mm
Straight Stitch

dk willow green 4mm
Ribbon Stitch

med yellow-green 4mm
Straight Stitch

dk purple 4mm
Straight Stitch

lt orange 4mm
Spiral Rose

black floss (1 strand)
French Knot

lt orange floss (1 strand)
Tack Stitch

lt yellow-green 4mm
Straight Stitch

Stitching order:

Use floss to Backstitch fence outline and to Stem Stitch stems. Work Ribbon Stitch and Straight Stitch leaves, including three bent ones.

For orchid and purple flowers, work Straight Stitch petals and buds. Use floss to work Straight Stitches between petals, add calyxes, and work Colonial Knot centers on full flowers. For tall pink buds, work Padded Straight Stitch (Straight Stitch over Straight Stitch). For each coral flower, work Straight Stitch petals and a French Knot center.

For the snail, work a Straight Stitch body, Spiral Rose shell, and French Knot eye.

Forget-Me-Nots

(see photo, page 19)

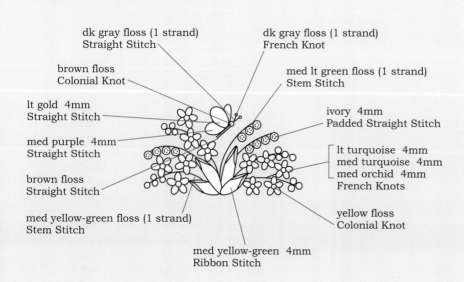

dk gray floss (1 strand)
Straight Stitch

dk gray floss (1 strand)
French Knot

brown floss
Colonial Knot

med lt green floss (1 strand)
Stem Stitch

lt gold 4mm
Straight Stitch

ivory 4mm
Padded Straight Stitch

med purple 4mm
Straight Stitch

lt turquoise 4mm
med turquoise 4mm
med orchid 4mm
French Knots

brown floss
Straight Stitch

yellow floss
Colonial Knot

med yellow-green floss (1 strand)
Stem Stitch

med yellow-green 4mm
Ribbon Stitch

Stitching order:

Use two color values of floss to Stem Stitch stems. Work Ribbon Stitch leaves. For the blue flowers and buds, work French Knots in a random color arrangement. Use floss to work Colonial Knot centers on full flowers.

For the white buds, work Padded Straight Stitch (Straight Stitch over French Knot). For the butterfly, use floss to work two Straight Stitches for body; add a Colonial Knot head and Straight Stitch with French Knot antennae. Work Straight Stitch wings with upper ones overlapping.

Fruit Basket

(see photo, page 20)

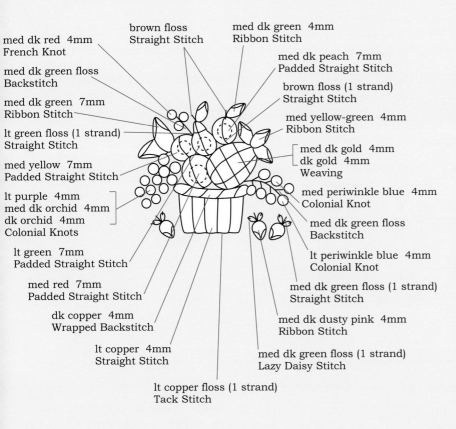

med dk red 4mm
French Knot

med dk green floss
Backstitch

med dk green 7mm
Ribbon Stitch

lt green floss (1 strand)
Straight Stitch

med yellow 7mm
Padded Straight Stitch

lt purple 4mm
med dk orchid 4mm
dk orchid 4mm
Colonial Knots

lt green 7mm
Padded Straight Stitch

med red 7mm
Padded Straight Stitch

dk copper 4mm
Wrapped Backstitch

lt copper 4mm
Straight Stitch

lt copper floss (1 strand)
Tack Stitch

brown floss
Straight Stitch

med dk green 4mm
Ribbon Stitch

med dk peach 7mm
Padded Straight Stitch

brown floss (1 strand)
Straight Stitch

med yellow-green 4mm
Ribbon Stitch

med dk gold 4mm
dk gold 4mm
Weaving

med periwinkle blue 4mm
Colonial Knot

med dk green floss
Backstitch

lt periwinkle blue 4mm
Colonial Knot

med dk green floss (1 strand)
Straight Stitch

med dk dusty pink 4mm
Ribbon Stitch

med dk green floss (1 strand)
Lazy Daisy Stitch

Stitching order:

Work basket with Straight Stitches, tacked in place; add a Wrapped Backstitch rim. Work Ribbon Stitch leaves. Use floss to Backstitch cherry and blueberry stems. For the grapes, work Colonial Knots in a random color arrangement. For the cherries, work French Knots.

For the grapefruit and peach, work Padded Straight Stitch (two Straight Stitches over one Colonial Knot); use floss to Straight Stitch a stem and a mid-section line on peach. For apple and pear, work Padded Straight Stitch (two Straight Stitches over one Colonial Knot); work a floss Straight Stitch to create pear shape and add a Straight Stitch stem.

For the pineapple, work the Weaving technique diagonally. Work Colonial Knots for the blueberries. Work Ribbon Stitch strawberries, each topped with a Straight Stitch stem and Lazy Daisy Stitch leaves.

Fruit Bowl

(see photo, page 19)

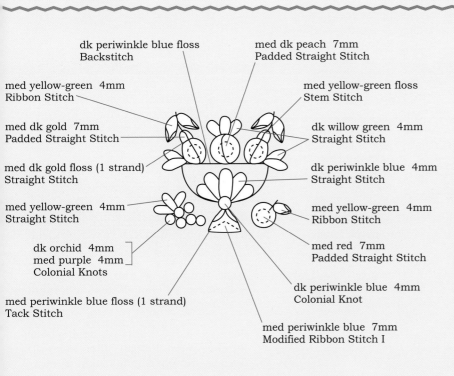

dk periwinkle blue floss
Backstitch

med yellow-green 4mm
Ribbon Stitch

med dk gold 7mm
Padded Straight Stitch

med dk gold floss (1 strand)
Straight Stitch

med yellow-green 4mm
Straight Stitch

dk orchid 4mm
med purple 4mm
Colonial Knots

med periwinkle blue floss (1 strand)
Tack Stitch

med dk peach 7mm
Padded Straight Stitch

med yellow-green floss
Stem Stitch

dk willow green 4mm
Straight Stitch

dk periwinkle blue 4mm
Straight Stitch

med yellow-green 4mm
Ribbon Stitch

med red 7mm
Padded Straight Stitch

dk periwinkle blue 4mm
Colonial Knot

med periwinkle blue 7mm
Modified Ribbon Stitch I

Stitching order:

Use floss to Backstitch outline of bowl. Work base with Modified Ribbon Stitch I and a Colonial Knot; add overlapping Straight Stitches for decoration.

For the orange, work Padded Straight Stitch (two Straight Stitches over one Colonial Knot). For each pear, work Padded Straight Stitch (two Straight Stitches over one Colonial Knot); work a floss Straight Stitch to create pear shape.

For the grapes, work Colonial Knots in a random color arrangement. For the apple, work Padded Straight Stitch (Straight Stitch over Colonial Knot). Use floss to Stem Stitch stems. Add Ribbon Stitch and Straight Stitch leaves.

Fruit Tiles

(see photo, back cover)

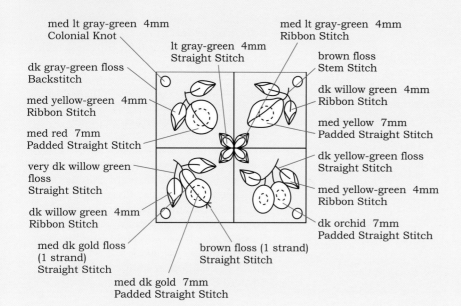

med lt gray-green 4mm
Colonial Knot

lt gray-green 4mm
Straight Stitch

med lt gray-green 4mm
Ribbon Stitch

dk gray-green floss
Backstitch

brown floss
Stem Stitch

med yellow-green 4mm
Ribbon Stitch

dk willow green 4mm
Ribbon Stitch

med red 7mm
Padded Straight Stitch

med yellow 7mm
Padded Straight Stitch

very dk willow green
floss
Straight Stitch

dk yellow-green floss
Straight Stitch

dk willow green 4mm
Ribbon Stitch

med yellow-green 4mm
Ribbon Stitch

med dk gold floss
(1 strand)
Straight Stitch

dk orchid 7mm
Padded Straight Stitch

brown floss (1 strand)
Straight Stitch

med dk gold 7mm
Padded Straight Stitch

Stitching order:

Use floss to Backstitch outlines. For the apple, lemon, and pear, work Padded Straight Stitch (two Straight Stitches over one Colonial Knot). Work floss Straight Stitch over pear to create shape. For the plums, work Padded Straight Stitch (Straight Stitch over Colonial Knot).

Work Ribbon Stitch leaves. Use floss to Stem Stitch and Straight Stitch fruit and leaf stems, extending stitching into leaves for midribs; add tuft to bottom of pear.

At center, work Straight Stitches on top of Ribbon Stitches. At corners work Colonial Knots.

Fruits All Around

(see photo, page 17)

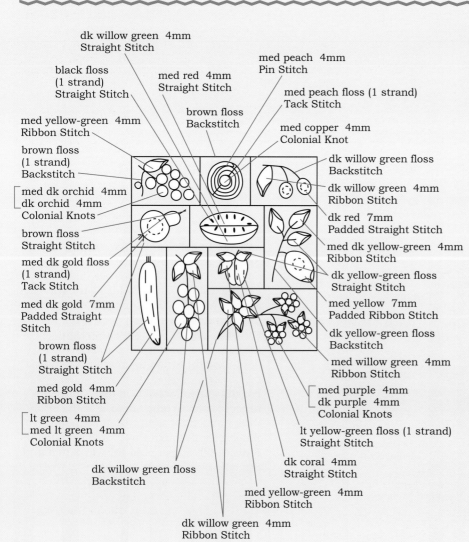

dk willow green 4mm
Straight Stitch

black floss
(1 strand)
Straight Stitch

med red 4mm
Straight Stitch

med peach 4mm
Pin Stitch

brown floss
Backstitch

med peach floss (1 strand)
Tack Stitch

med yellow-green 4mm
Ribbon Stitch

med copper 4mm
Colonial Knot

brown floss
(1 strand)
Backstitch

dk willow green floss
Backstitch

med dk orchid 4mm
dk orchid 4mm
Colonial Knots

dk willow green 4mm
Ribbon Stitch

brown floss
Straight Stitch

dk red 7mm
Padded Straight Stitch

med dk gold floss
(1 strand)
Tack Stitch

med dk yellow-green 4mm
Ribbon Stitch

med dk gold 7mm
Padded Straight
Stitch

dk yellow-green floss
Straight Stitch

med yellow 7mm
Padded Ribbon Stitch

brown floss
(1 strand)
Straight Stitch

dk yellow-green floss
Backstitch

med gold 4mm
Ribbon Stitch

med willow green 4mm
Ribbon Stitch

lt green 4mm
med lt green 4mm
Colonial Knots

med purple 4mm
dk purple 4mm
Colonial Knots

lt yellow-green floss (1 strand)
Straight Stitch

dk willow green floss
Backstitch

dk coral 4mm
Straight Stitch

med yellow-green 4mm
Ribbon Stitch

dk willow green 4mm
Ribbon Stitch

Stitching order:

Use floss to Backstitch outlines. For purple grapes, work Colonial Knots in a random color arrangement. Use floss to Straight Stitch stem and Backstitch tendril. Work a Ribbon Stitch leaf. For the cut peach, work a Pin Stitch with a Colonial Knot at center.

For cherries, lemon, green grapes, and berries, use floss to Backstitch stems. Work Ribbon Stitch leaves, then Straight Stitch midribs on lemon leaves with floss. For cherries, work Padded Straight Stitch (Straight Stitch over French Knot). For pear, work Padded Straight Stitch (Straight Stitch over Colonial Knot); work floss Straight Stitch over pear to create shape. Use floss to Straight Stitch stem and tuft at base.

For watermelon, work two red and one green Straight Stitches. Use floss to Straight Stitch seeds. For lemon, work Padded Ribbon Stitch (Ribbon Stitch over Colonial Knot). For banana, work a Ribbon Stitch; use floss to Straight Stitch stem, grain marks, and tip. For green grapes, work Colonial Knots in a random color arrangement.

For strawberry, work overlapping Straight Stitches. Work Ribbon Stitch leaves. Use floss to Straight Stitch stem and seed marks. For berries, work Colonial Knots in a random color arrangement.

Fruits & Flowers

(see photo, front cover)

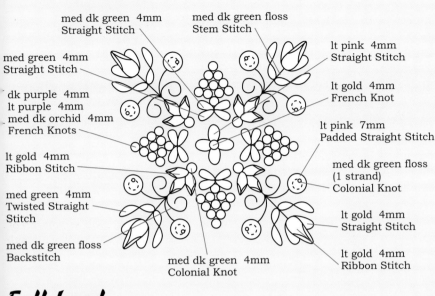

med dk green 4mm
Straight Stitch

med dk green floss
Stem Stitch

med green 4mm
Straight Stitch

lt pink 4mm
Straight Stitch

dk purple 4mm
lt purple 4mm
med dk orchid 4mm
French Knots

lt gold 4mm
French Knot

lt gold 4mm
Ribbon Stitch

lt pink 7mm
Padded Straight Stitch

med dk green floss
(1 strand)
Colonial Knot

med green 4mm
Twisted Straight
Stitch

med dk green floss
Backstitch

lt gold 4mm
Straight Stitch

med dk green 4mm
Colonial Knot

lt gold 4mm
Ribbon Stitch

Stitching order:

Use floss to Stem Stitch stems and Backstitch curliques. Work Twisted Straight Stitch and Straight Stitch leaves. Work each bunch of French Knot grapes in the same random color arrangement. For center flower, work Straight Stitch petals with a French Knot center.

For each corner motif, begin at the outside edge and work two Straight Stitches with a Ribbon Stitch centered on top. Work Padded Straight Stitch (Straight Stitch over Colonial Knot) for berries; use floss to work a Colonial Knot at bottom of each berry. Work three overlapping Ribbon Stitches below curliques and add a Colonial Knot at base.

Full Load

(see photo, page 19)

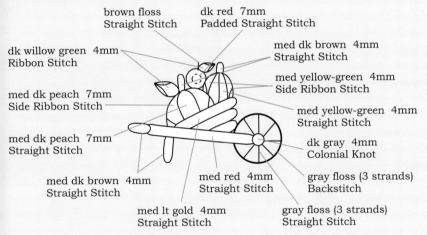

brown floss
Straight Stitch

dk red 7mm
Padded Straight Stitch

dk willow green 4mm
Ribbon Stitch

med dk brown 4mm
Straight Stitch

med yellow-green 4mm
Side Ribbon Stitch

med dk peach 7mm
Side Ribbon Stitch

med yellow-green 4mm
Straight Stitch

med dk peach 7mm
Straight Stitch

dk gray 4mm
Colonial Knot

med dk brown 4mm
Straight Stitch

med red 4mm
Straight Stitch

gray floss (3 strands)
Backstitch

med lt gold 4mm
Straight Stitch

gray floss (3 strands)
Straight Stitch

Stitching order:

For pumpkin, work two Side Ribbon Stitches and a Straight Stitch centered on top. For apple, work a Padded Straight Stitch (Straight Stitch over Colonial Knot). For watermelon, work Side Ribbon Stitches on outside edges with two Straight Stitches in the middle.

Work Straight Stitch stems on pumpkin and watermelon and Ribbon Stitch leaves on pumpkin and apple. Use floss to Straight Stitch apple stem. Work Straight Stitches for basket, base of wheelbarrow, handle, and support. Use floss to Backstitch and Straight Stitch wheel. Work a Colonial Knot at wheel center.

Note: Design is stitched on an angle in photo.

Garden Gate

(see photo, front cover)

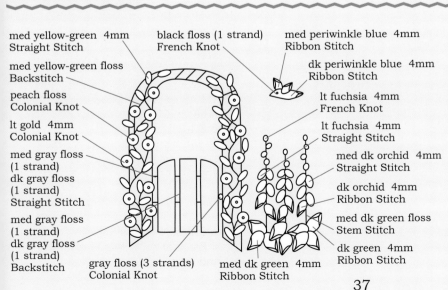

med yellow-green 4mm
Straight Stitch

black floss (1 strand)
French Knot

med periwinkle blue 4mm
Ribbon Stitch

med yellow-green floss
Backstitch

dk periwinkle blue 4mm
Ribbon Stitch

peach floss
Colonial Knot

lt fuchsia 4mm
French Knot

lt gold 4mm
Colonial Knot

lt fuchsia 4mm
Straight Stitch

med gray floss
(1 strand)
dk gray floss
(1 strand)
Straight Stitch

med dk orchid 4mm
Straight Stitch

dk orchid 4mm
Ribbon Stitch

med gray floss
(1 strand)
dk gray floss
(1 strand)
Backstitch

med dk green floss
Stem Stitch

dk green 4mm
Ribbon Stitch

gray floss (3 strands)
Colonial Knot

med dk green 4mm
Ribbon Stitch

Stitching order:

Use blended floss to Backstitch and Straight Stitch trellis and gate; Backstitch vines and Stem Stitch flower stems. Use floss to work Colonial Knot gate latch. Work Straight Stitch and Ribbon Stitch leaves.

For each vine flower, work a loose Colonial Knot with a floss Colonial Knot centered on top. For the tall flowers work Ribbon Stitches at bottom, then Straight Stitches toward middle, and French Knots at top. For the bluebird, work Ribbon Stitches; add a floss French Knot eye.

Garden Medley

(see photo, page 17)

Stitching order:

Use floss to Backstitch outlines. For the artichoke, pepper, and squash, work overlapping Straight Stitches. Use floss to Straight Stitch midribs to artichoke, stems to pepper and squash, and tuft at base of squash.

For the beet, work a loose Colonial Knot; add Straight Stitch leaves. For the eggplant, work Padded Straight Stitch (Straight Stitch over Colonial Knot), tacking edges to create shape; add Ribbon Stitch leaves. For the pumpkin, work overlapping Straight Stitches; add Ribbon Stitch leaves. For the carrot, work overlapping

Ribbon Stitches. Use floss to Straight Stitch and Backstitch stems and greenery on beet, eggplant, pumpkin, and carrot.

For the asparagus, work a Modified Straight Stitch; use floss to work Lazy Daisy leaves. For the turnip, work a Padded Ribbon Stitch (Ribbon Stitch over Colonial Knot) and use floss to Backstitch stems and Straight Stitch coloration at top; add Straight Stitch leaves. For the corn, work Ribbon Stitch leaves covered with Colonial Knot kernels worked with floss; work Bent Straight Stitch husks and use floss to Straight Stitch stem.

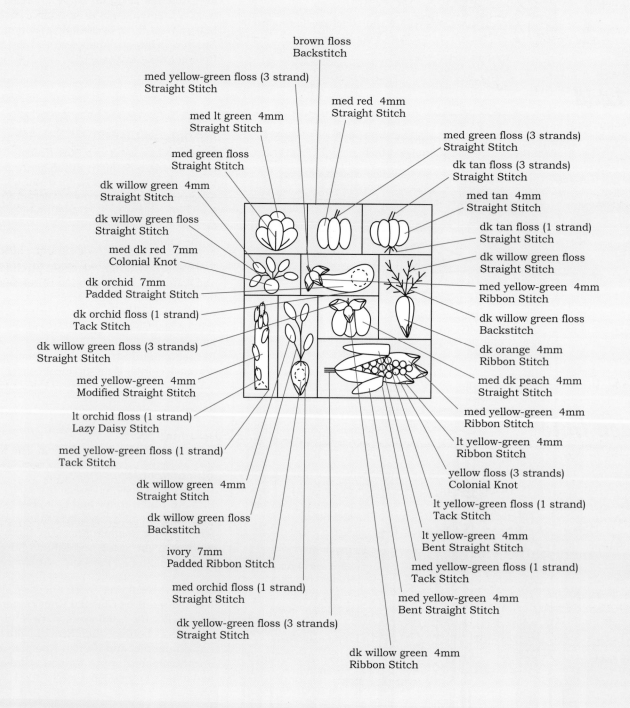

brown floss
Backstitch

med yellow-green floss (3 strand)
Straight Stitch

med lt green 4mm
Straight Stitch

med red 4mm
Straight Stitch

med green floss
Straight Stitch

med green floss (3 strands)
Straight Stitch

dk willow green 4mm
Straight Stitch

dk tan floss (3 strands)
Straight Stitch

dk willow green floss
Straight Stitch

med tan 4mm
Straight Stitch

med dk red 7mm
Colonial Knot

dk tan floss (1 strand)
Straight Stitch

dk orchid 7mm
Padded Straight Stitch

dk willow green floss
Straight Stitch

dk orchid floss (1 strand)
Tack Stitch

med yellow-green 4mm
Ribbon Stitch

dk willow green floss (3 strands)
Straight Stitch

dk willow green floss
Backstitch

med yellow-green 4mm
Modified Straight Stitch

dk orange 4mm
Ribbon Stitch

lt orchid floss (1 strand)
Lazy Daisy Stitch

med dk peach 4mm
Straight Stitch

med yellow-green floss (1 strand)
Tack Stitch

med yellow-green 4mm
Ribbon Stitch

dk willow green 4mm
Straight Stitch

lt yellow-green 4mm
Ribbon Stitch

dk willow green floss
Backstitch

yellow floss (3 strands)
Colonial Knot

ivory 7mm
Padded Ribbon Stitch

lt yellow-green floss (1 strand)
Tack Stitch

med orchid floss (1 strand)
Straight Stitch

lt yellow-green 4mm
Bent Straight Stitch

dk yellow-green floss (3 strands)
Straight Stitch

med yellow-green floss (1 strand)
Tack Stitch

med yellow-green 4mm
Bent Straight Stitch

dk willow green 4mm
Ribbon Stitch

38

Gardening Whatnots

(see photo, page 20)

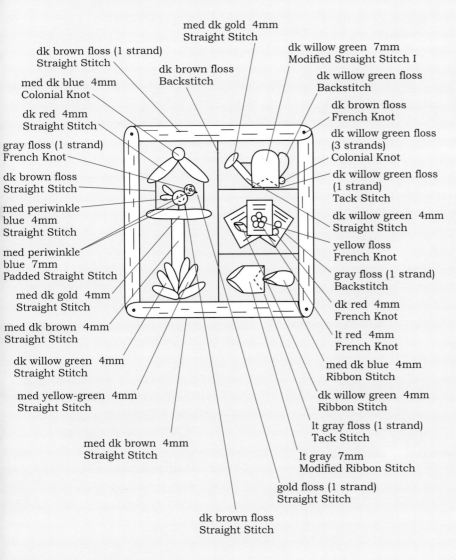

med dk gold 4mm
Straight Stitch

dk brown floss (1 strand)
Straight Stitch

dk brown floss
Backstitch

dk willow green 7mm
Modified Straight Stitch I

med dk blue 4mm
Colonial Knot

dk willow green floss
Backstitch

dk red 4mm
Straight Stitch

dk brown floss
French Knot

gray floss (1 strand)
French Knot

dk willow green floss
(3 strands)
Colonial Knot

dk brown floss
Straight Stitch

dk willow green floss
(1 strand)
Tack Stitch

med periwinkle
blue 4mm
Straight Stitch

dk willow green 4mm
Straight Stitch

med periwinkle
blue 7mm
Padded Straight Stitch

yellow floss
French Knot

med dk gold 4mm
Straight Stitch

gray floss (1 strand)
Backstitch

med dk brown 4mm
Straight Stitch

dk red 4mm
French Knot

dk willow green 4mm
Straight Stitch

lt red 4mm
French Knot

med yellow-green 4mm
Straight Stitch

med dk blue 4mm
Ribbon Stitch

dk willow green 4mm
Ribbon Stitch

med dk brown 4mm
Straight Stitch

lt gray floss (1 strand)
Tack Stitch

lt gray 7mm
Modified Ribbon Stitch

gold floss (1 strand)
Straight Stitch

dk brown floss
Straight Stitch

Stitching order:
Use floss to Backstitch separating outlines. For the birdhouse, work Straight Stitch for the pole, leaves, floor, and roof. For the bird, work Padded Straight Stitch (Straight Stitch over Colonial Knot) for body and head and Straight Stitches for tail; use floss to Straight Stitch beak, feet, and French Knot eye. Use floss to Straight Stitch sides of house. Add a Colonial Knot to peak of roof.

For watering can, work Modified Straight Stitch I; tack can along edges to create shape. For the spout and sprinkler, work Straight Stitches. Use floss to Backstitch handle and brace; add a Colonial Knot at base of handle.

For seed packets, use floss to Backstitch packets and printing. Work a Ribbon Stitch leaf, French Knot flower, and French Knot berries. Work a floss French Knot at center of flower.

For trowel, work a Modified Ribbon Stitch, tacked at sides to create shape. Work a Ribbon Stitch handle.

For the frame, work long Straight Stitches; use floss to anchor each side with random Straight Stitches, adding a French Knot at each corner.

Garlic & Peppers

(see photo, page 17)

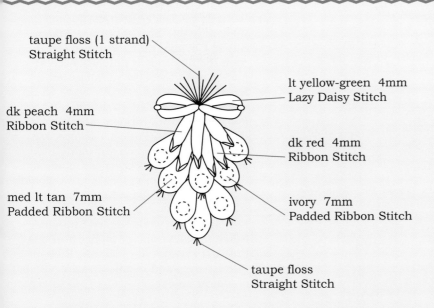

taupe floss (1 strand)
Straight Stitch

lt yellow-green 4mm
Lazy Daisy Stitch

dk peach 4mm
Ribbon Stitch

dk red 4mm
Ribbon Stitch

med lt tan 7mm
Padded Ribbon Stitch

ivory 7mm
Padded Ribbon Stitch

taupe floss
Straight Stitch

Stitching order:
For garlic, work Padded Ribbon Stitch (Ribbon Stitch over Colonial Knot). Use floss to Straight Stitch rootlets at base of each garlic.

Work Ribbon Stitch peppers. Add a Lazy Daisy bow and use floss to Straight Stitch stem ends at top.

Halloween Whatnots

(see photo, page 20)

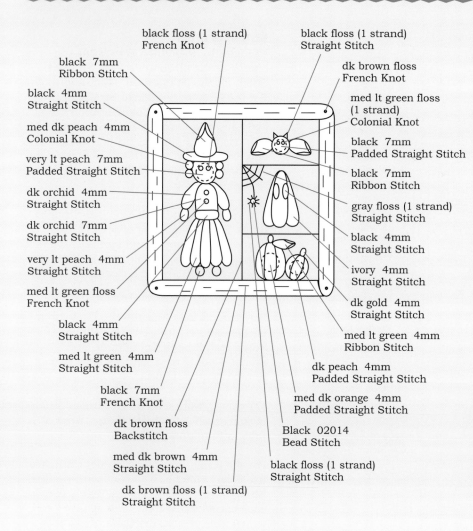

black floss (1 strand)
French Knot

black 7mm
Ribbon Stitch

black 4mm
Straight Stitch

med dk peach 4mm
Colonial Knot

very lt peach 7mm
Padded Straight Stitch

dk orchid 4mm
Straight Stitch

dk orchid 7mm
Straight Stitch

very lt peach 4mm
Straight Stitch

med lt green floss
French Knot

black 4mm
Straight Stitch

med lt green 4mm
Straight Stitch

black 7mm
French Knot

dk brown floss
Backstitch

med dk brown 4mm
Straight Stitch

dk brown floss (1 strand)
Straight Stitch

black floss (1 strand)
Straight Stitch

dk brown floss
French Knot

med lt green floss
(1 strand)
Colonial Knot

black 7mm
Padded Straight Stitch

black 7mm
Ribbon Stitch

gray floss (1 strand)
Straight Stitch

black 4mm
Straight Stitch

ivory 4mm
Straight Stitch

dk gold 4mm
Straight Stitch

med lt green 4mm
Ribbon Stitch

dk peach 4mm
Padded Straight Stitch

med dk orange 4mm
Padded Straight Stitch

Black 02014
Bead Stitch

black floss (1 strand)
Straight Stitch

Stitching order:

Use floss to Backstitch outlines. For the witch, work Padded Straight Stitch (Straight Stitch over Colonial Knot) for the face and Straight Stitches for the hands. Work Straight Stitches for dress, overlapping them on skirt. Work Colonial Knot hair and French Knot feet. Work a Straight Stitch belt and hat brim and a Ribbon Stitch hat crown. Use floss to work French Knot eyes and buttons.

For the bat, work a Padded Straight Stitch (Straight Stitch over Colonial Knot) head and Ribbon Stitch wings. Use floss to Straight Stitch ears and work Colonial Knot eyes.

For the ghost, work overlapping Straight Stitches for body; cover with two more Straight Stitches for eyes. Use floss to Straight Stitch spider and web. Attach a seed bead for spider body.

For pumpkins, work Padded Straight Stitch (three Straight Stitches over one Colonial Knot). Add Straight Stitch stems and a Ribbon Stitch leaf.

For the frame, work long Straight Stitches; use floss to anchor each side with random Straight Stitches, adding a French Knot at each corner.

Harvest Centerpiece

(see photo, page 18)

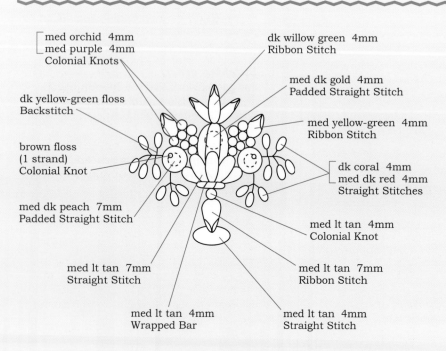

med orchid 4mm
med purple 4mm
Colonial Knots

dk yellow-green floss
Backstitch

brown floss
(1 strand)
Colonial Knot

med dk peach 7mm
Padded Straight Stitch

med lt tan 7mm
Straight Stitch

med lt tan 4mm
Wrapped Bar

dk willow green 4mm
Ribbon Stitch

med dk gold 4mm
Padded Straight Stitch

med yellow-green 4mm
Ribbon Stitch

dk coral 4mm
med dk red 4mm
Straight Stitches

med lt tan 4mm
Colonial Knot

med lt tan 7mm
Ribbon Stitch

med lt tan 4mm
Straight Stitch

Stitching order:

Work flower holder from the bottom upward with a Straight Stitch, Ribbon Stitch, Colonial Knot, Wrapped Bar, and overlapping Straight Stitches (except middle one). Use floss to Backstitch stems.

For berries, work Straight Stitches with two color values. For each orange, work a Padded Straight Stitch (Straight Stitch over Colonial Knot); use floss to add a Colonial Knot. For grapes, work Colonial Knots with two color values.

For pineapple, work Padded Straight Stitch (three Straight Stitches over one Colonial Knot). Add remaining Ribbon Stitch leaves and middle Straight Stitch on flower holder.

Harvest Cornucopia

(see photo, page 20)

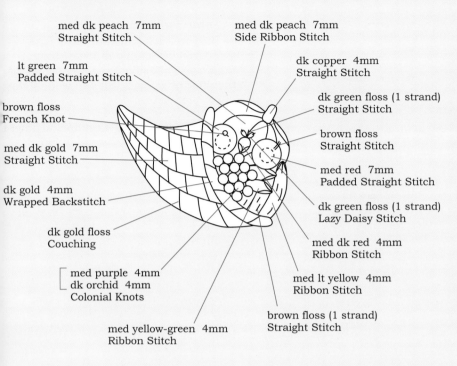

med dk peach 7mm
Straight Stitch

lt green 7mm
Padded Straight Stitch

brown floss
French Knot

med dk gold 7mm
Straight Stitch

dk gold 4mm
Wrapped Backstitch

dk gold floss
Couching

med purple 4mm
dk orchid 4mm
Colonial Knots

med yellow-green 4mm
Ribbon Stitch

med dk peach 7mm
Side Ribbon Stitch

dk copper 4mm
Straight Stitch

dk green floss (1 strand)
Straight Stitch

brown floss
Straight Stitch

med red 7mm
Padded Straight Stitch

dk green floss (1 strand)
Lazy Daisy Stitch

med dk red 4mm
Ribbon Stitch

med lt yellow 4mm
Ribbon Stitch

brown floss (1 strand)
Straight Stitch

Stitching order:
Work long, loose Straight Stitches for length of cornucopia; use floss to couch down the stitches in a random pattern. Work Wrapped Backstitch for rim.

For pumpkin, work a Side Ribbon Stitch on each outside edge and three Straight Stitches centered on top. Add a Straight Stitch stem. For apples, work Padded Straight Stitch (Straight Stitch over Colonial Knot); use floss to add a French Knot to end of green apple and a Straight Stitch stem to end of red apple.

For strawberry, work a Ribbon Stitch; use floss to top with a Straight Stitch stem and Lazy Daisy leaves. For bananas, work Ribbon Stitches; use floss to work random Straight Stitches along lengths. For grapes, work Colonial Knots in a random color arrangement; add Ribbon Stitch leaves.

Home Tweet Home

(see photo, page 17)

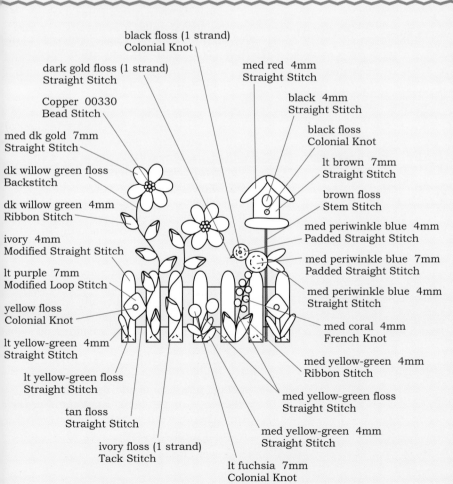

black floss (1 strand)
Colonial Knot

dark gold floss (1 strand)
Straight Stitch

Copper 00330
Bead Stitch

med dk gold 7mm
Straight Stitch

dk willow green floss
Backstitch

dk willow green 4mm
Ribbon Stitch

ivory 4mm
Modified Straight Stitch

lt purple 7mm
Modified Loop Stitch

yellow floss
Colonial Knot

lt yellow-green 4mm
Straight Stitch

lt yellow-green floss
Straight Stitch

tan floss
Straight Stitch

ivory floss (1 strand)
Tack Stitch

med red 4mm
Straight Stitch

black 4mm
Straight Stitch

black floss
Colonial Knot

lt brown 7mm
Straight Stitch

brown floss
Stem Stitch

med periwinkle blue 4mm
Padded Straight Stitch

med periwinkle blue 7mm
Padded Straight Stitch

med periwinkle blue 4mm
Straight Stitch

med coral 4mm
French Knot

med yellow-green 4mm
Ribbon Stitch

med yellow-green floss
Straight Stitch

med yellow-green 4mm
Straight Stitch

lt fuchsia 7mm
Colonial Knot

Stitching order:
Work Modified Straight Stitches for the fence; use floss to tack edges in place and Straight Stitch crossbars. Use floss to Backstitch and Straight Stitch stems. Work Ribbon Stitch and Straight Stitch leaves.

For the purple flower at each end, work a Modified Loop Stitch; use floss to work a Colonial Knot at center. For each daisy-like flower, work loose Straight Stitch petals and attach seed beads at center. For the short flowers, work Colonial Knots. For the tall flower spike, work French Knots.

Use floss to work two or three parallel rows of Stem Stitch for the birdhouse pole. For bird, work Padded Straight Stitch (Straight Stitch over Colonial Knot) for body and head and Straight Stitch tail feathers. Use floss to Straight Stitch beak and make a Colonial Knot eye.

For front of birdhouse, work a Straight Stitch; cover ends with a Straight Stitch roof and base. Work a Straight Stitch for opening and use floss to work a Colonial Knot for perch.

Hyacinths

(see photo, page 17)

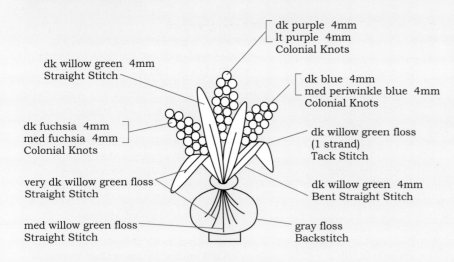

dk purple 4mm
lt purple 4mm
Colonial Knots

dk willow green 4mm
Straight Stitch

dk blue 4mm
med periwinkle blue 4mm
Colonial Knots

dk fuchsia 4mm
med fuchsia 4mm
Colonial Knots

dk willow green floss
(1 strand)
Tack Stitch

very dk willow green floss
Straight Stitch

dk willow green 4mm
Bent Straight Stitch

med willow green floss
Straight Stitch

gray floss
Backstitch

Stitching order:

Use floss to Backstitch outline of vase. Work Straight Stitch and Bent Straight Stitch leaves. Use floss to add a Straight Stitch midrib to each leaf and work stems in two color values.

Work each hyacinth in a random arrangement with two color values of Colonial Knots.

Jacobean Heart

(see photo, front cover)

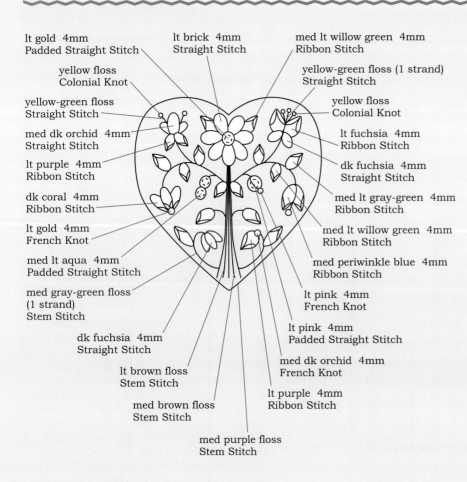

lt gold 4mm
Padded Straight Stitch

lt brick 4mm
Straight Stitch

med lt willow green 4mm
Ribbon Stitch

yellow floss
Colonial Knot

yellow-green floss (1 strand)
Straight Stitch

yellow-green floss
Straight Stitch

yellow floss
Colonial Knot

med dk orchid 4mm
Straight Stitch

lt fuchsia 4mm
Ribbon Stitch

lt purple 4mm
Ribbon Stitch

dk fuchsia 4mm
Straight Stitch

dk coral 4mm
Ribbon Stitch

med lt gray-green 4mm
Ribbon Stitch

lt gold 4mm
French Knot

med lt willow green 4mm
Ribbon Stitch

med lt aqua 4mm
Padded Straight Stitch

med periwinkle blue 4mm
Ribbon Stitch

med gray-green floss
(1 strand)
Stem Stitch

lt pink 4mm
French Knot

lt pink 4mm
Padded Straight Stitch

dk fuchsia 4mm
Straight Stitch

med dk orchid 4mm
French Knot

lt brown floss
Stem Stitch

med brown floss
Stem Stitch

lt purple 4mm
Ribbon Stitch

med purple floss
Stem Stitch

Stitching order:

Use floss to Stem Stitch heart outline, all stems, and parallel rows for main trunk. Work Ribbon Stitch Leaves. For the center top flower, work Straight Stitch petals and a Padded Straight Stitch (Straight Stitch over French Knot) at center.

Working down the left side, for purple flower, work Ribbon Stitch and Straight Stitch petals; use floss to add Straight Stitch stamens with Colonial Knot ends. For coral flower, work overlapping Ribbon Stitches with a French Knot at tip. For aqua flower, work Padded Straight Stitch (Straight Stitch over French Knot). For fuchsia flower, work overlapping Straight Stitches.

Working down the right side, for fuchsia flower, work Straight Stitch and Ribbon Stitch petals; use floss to add Straight Stitch stamens with Colonial Knots at ends. For pink bud, work Padded Straight Stitch (two Straight Stitches over one Colonial Knot) with a French Knot at tip. For the blue flower, work Ribbon Stitch petals; use floss to add Straight Stitch stamen with a Colonial Knot end. For the orchid bud, work a Ribbon Stitch with a French Knot at base.

Jacobean Motif

(see photo, page 17)

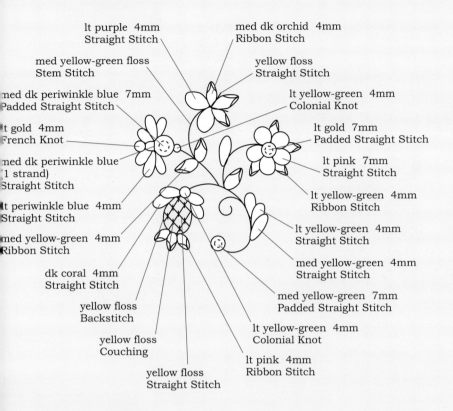

lt purple 4mm
Straight Stitch

med yellow-green floss
Stem Stitch

med dk periwinkle blue 7mm
Padded Straight Stitch

lt gold 4mm
French Knot

med dk periwinkle blue
(1 strand)
Straight Stitch

lt periwinkle blue 4mm
Straight Stitch

med yellow-green 4mm
Ribbon Stitch

dk coral 4mm
Straight Stitch

yellow floss
Backstitch

yellow floss
Couching

yellow floss
Straight Stitch

med dk orchid 4mm
Ribbon Stitch

yellow floss
Straight Stitch

lt yellow-green 4mm
Colonial Knot

lt gold 7mm
Padded Straight Stitch

lt pink 7mm
Straight Stitch

lt yellow-green 4mm
Ribbon Stitch

lt yellow-green 4mm
Straight Stitch

med yellow-green 4mm
Straight Stitch

med yellow-green 7mm
Padded Straight Stitch

lt yellow-green 4mm
Colonial Knot

lt pink 4mm
Ribbon Stitch

Stitching order:
Use floss to Stem Stitch stems. Add Ribbon Stitch and Straight Stitch leaves. Work a Padded Straight Stitch (Straight Stitch over Colonial Knot) over stem end.

For the yellow flower, use floss to work diagonal Straight Stitches; couch down intersections and Backstitch outline. Work Straight Stitch petals, a Colonial Knot base, and three Ribbon Stitches at tip.

For the blue flower, work a Padded Straight Stitch (Straight Stitch over Colonial Knot); work a floss Straight Stitch to create shape. Add Straight Stitch side petals, a French Knot at center tip, and a Colonial Knot base.

For the purple flower, work Straight Stitch and Ribbon Stitch petals. Use floss to work Straight Stitches between petals. For the pink flower, work loose Straight Stitch petals around a Padded Straight Stitch (Straight Stitch over Colonial Knot); add Ribbon Stitches between petals.

Jacobean Tree

(see photo, page 19)

dk willow green floss
Backstitch

med willow green 4mm
Ribbon Stitch

med dk gold 4mm
Straight Stitch

med dusty pink 4mm
Colonial Knot

med dusty pink floss
(1 strand)
Straight Stitch

lt periwinkle blue 4mm
Padded Straight Stitch

lt yellow-green 4mm
Colonial Knot

very lt fuchsia 4mm
Side Ribbon Stitch

lt fuchsia 4mm
Ribbon Stitch

lt purple 7mm
Padded Straight Stitch

med orchid 7mm
Padded Straight Stitch

dk yellow-green floss
Backstitch

lt yellow-green floss
Backstitch

med dk periwinkle blue 7mm
Padded Straight Stitch

med dk gold floss
Straight Stitch

med dk gold 4mm
French Knot

lt fuchsia 4mm
Straight Stitch

lt yellow-green 4mm
Colonial Knot

med lt gray-green 7mm
Ribbon Stitch

lt yellow-green 4mm
Ribbon Stitch

med dusty pink 4mm
Straight Stitch

med dk gold 7mm
Colonial Knot

med willow green 4mm
Ribbon Stitch

lt periwinkle blue 7mm
Modified Loop Stitch

lt purple 7mm
French Knot

med lt brown floss
Stem Stitch

dk willow green floss (1 strand)
Straight Stitch

Stitching order:
Use floss to Backstitch hills and Stem Stitch main branch with parallel rows; Backstitch stems and curliques. Add Ribbon Stitch leaves; use floss to Straight Stitch midribs to some leaves.

For the left fuchsia flower, work one Ribbon Stitch and two Side Ribbon Stitches; add a Colonial Knot base. For the blue bud, work a Padded Straight Stitch (Straight Stitch over Colonial Knot) topped with a Padded Straight Stitch (Straight Stitch over French Knot). For the gold flower work Straight Stitch petals around a Colonial Knot; use floss to Straight Stitch stamens. For purple berries, work Padded Straight Stitch (Straight Stitch over Colonial Knot) in two color values. For the right fuchsia flower, work Straight Stitch petals with a Colonial Knot base; use floss to work Straight Stitches between petals; add French Knots at stem ends. For the dusty pink flower, work three overlapping Straight Stitches; add Ribbon Stitch leaves. For the blue flower, work Modified Loop Stitch with a French Knot at center. For the yellow flower, work a loose Colonial Knot.

Knot Garden

(see photo, page 19)

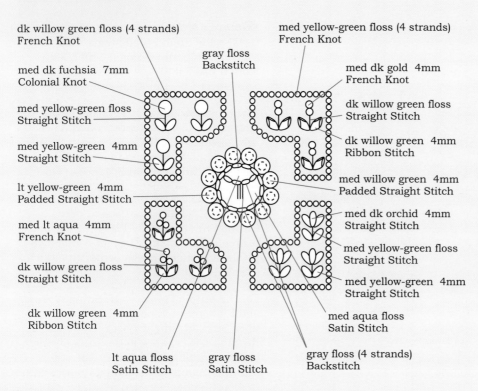

dk willow green floss (4 strands)
French Knot

med dk fuchsia 7mm
Colonial Knot

med yellow-green floss
Straight Stitch

med yellow-green 4mm
Straight Stitch

lt yellow-green 4mm
Padded Straight Stitch

med lt aqua 4mm
French Knot

dk willow green floss
Straight Stitch

dk willow green 4mm
Ribbon Stitch

gray floss
Backstitch

med yellow-green floss (4 strands)
French Knot

med dk gold 4mm
French Knot

dk willow green floss
Straight Stitch

dk willow green 4mm
Ribbon Stitch

med willow green 4mm
Padded Straight Stitch

med dk orchid 4mm
Straight Stitch

med yellow-green floss
Straight Stitch

med yellow-green 4mm
Straight Stitch

med aqua floss
Satin Stitch

lt aqua floss
Satin Stitch

gray floss
Satin Stitch

gray floss (4 strands)
Backstitch

Stitching order:

Use floss to outline each corner with French Knots and Straight Stitch the stems within each corner. Work Straight Stitch or Ribbon Stitch leaves.

For the fuchsia flowers, work Colonial Knots. For the gold and aqua flowers, work French Knots. For the orchid flowers, work overlapping Straight Stitches.

For the center motif, use floss to Backstitch the fountain (two strands for top curve and four strands for remaining outlines). Use floss to Satin Stitch the pedestal and the water. Work Padded Straight Stitches (Straight Stitch over Colonial Knot) around fountain in alternating colors.

Memories of Deerfield

(see photo, page 18)

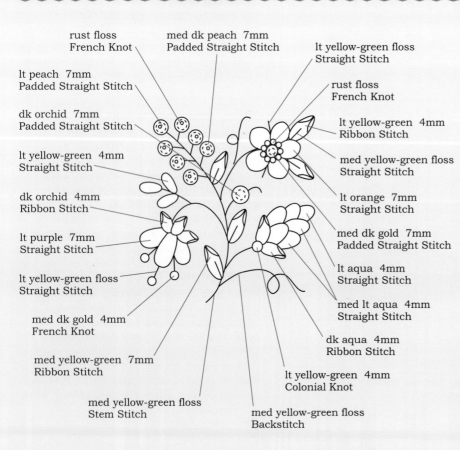

rust floss
French Knot

lt peach 7mm
Padded Straight Stitch

dk orchid 7mm
Padded Straight Stitch

lt yellow-green 4mm
Straight Stitch

dk orchid 4mm
Ribbon Stitch

lt purple 7mm
Straight Stitch

lt yellow-green floss
Straight Stitch

med dk gold 4mm
French Knot

med yellow-green 7mm
Ribbon Stitch

med yellow-green floss
Stem Stitch

med dk peach 7mm
Padded Straight Stitch

med yellow-green floss
Backstitch

lt yellow-green floss
Straight Stitch

rust floss
French Knot

lt yellow-green 4mm
Ribbon Stitch

med yellow-green floss
Straight Stitch

lt orange 7mm
Straight Stitch

med dk gold 7mm
Padded Straight Stitch

lt aqua 4mm
Straight Stitch

med lt aqua 4mm
Straight Stitch

dk aqua 4mm
Ribbon Stitch

lt yellow-green 4mm
Colonial Knot

Stitching order:

Use floss to Stem Stitch stems and Backstitch tendrils. Work Straight Stitch and Ribbon Stitch leaves. Use floss to Straight Stitch midribs on some leaves.

For the purple/orchid flower, work Straight Stitch and Ribbon Stitch petals. Add floss Straight Stitch stamens. Work a French Knot at end of each stamen. For orchid bud, work a Padded Straight Stitch (Straight Stitch over Colonial Knot).

For the peach berries, work Padded Straight Stitch (Straight Stitch over Colonial Knot); use floss to add a French Knot to each one. For the orange flower, work loose Straight Stitch petals; add a Padded Straight Stitch (Straight Stitch over Colonial Knot) at center. Use floss to work Straight Stitches between petals and French Knots around center.

For the aqua flower, begin at the tip and work overlapping Straight Stitches; work two Ribbon Stitches and a Colonial Knot at base.

Mille Fleur I

(see photo, front cover)

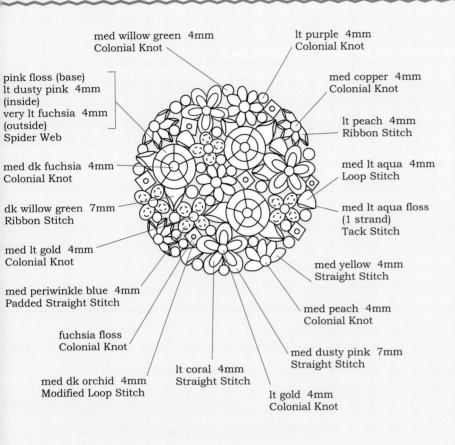

med willow green 4mm
Colonial Knot

lt purple 4mm
Colonial Knot

med copper 4mm
Colonial Knot

pink floss (base)
lt dusty pink 4mm
(inside)
very lt fuchsia 4mm
(outside)
Spider Web

lt peach 4mm
Ribbon Stitch

med dk fuchsia 4mm
Colonial Knot

med lt aqua 4mm
Loop Stitch

dk willow green 7mm
Ribbon Stitch

med lt aqua floss
(1 strand)
Tack Stitch

med lt gold 4mm
Colonial Knot

med periwinkle blue 4mm
Padded Straight Stitch

med yellow 4mm
Straight Stitch

fuchsia floss
Colonial Knot

med peach 4mm
Colonial Knot

med dusty pink 7mm
Straight Stitch

med dk orchid 4mm
Modified Loop Stitch

lt coral 4mm
Straight Stitch

lt gold 4mm
Colonial Knot

Stitching order:
This overall pattern is a mixture of stitches in a random color arrangement to fill the entire shape. Work the larger elements first, then the smaller ones.

For the round pink flowers, work Spider Web, using two color values for the weaving and a Colonial Knot at center. For the daisy-like pink flowers, work Straight Stitches over Straight Stitches for each petal and a Colonial Knot at center.

Work all Ribbon Stitch leaves. For the yellow daisies work Straight Stitch petals and for the peach daisies work Ribbon Stitch petals; add Colonial Knots at centers.

For the blue flowers, work Padded Straight Stitch (Straight Stitch over Straight Stitch) petals and a Colonial Knot at center. For the aqua buds, work Loop Stitch. For orchid flowers, work Modified Loop Stitch, held down with a floss Colonial Knot. Fill in remaining spaces with purple and green Colonial Knots.

Mille Fleur II

(see photo, page 17)

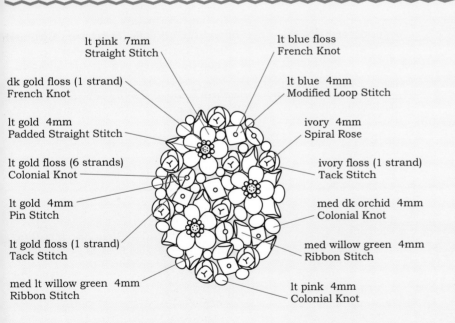

lt pink 7mm
Straight Stitch

lt blue floss
French Knot

dk gold floss (1 strand)
French Knot

lt blue 4mm
Modified Loop Stitch

lt gold 4mm
Padded Straight Stitch

ivory 4mm
Spiral Rose

lt gold floss (6 strands)
Colonial Knot

ivory floss (1 strand)
Tack Stitch

lt gold 4mm
Pin Stitch

med dk orchid 4mm
Colonial Knot

lt gold floss (1 strand)
Tack Stitch

med willow green 4mm
Ribbon Stitch

med lt willow green 4mm
Ribbon Stitch

lt pink 4mm
Colonial Knot

Stitching order:
This overall pattern is a mixture of stitches in a random color arrangement to fill the entire shape. Work the larger elements first, then the smaller ones.

For the pink flowers, work loose Straight Stitch petals and a Padded Straight Stitch (Straight Stitch over Colonial Knot) at center. Use floss to surround center with French Knots.

Using two color values, work all leaves in Ribbon Stitch. For each ivory flower, work a Spiral Rose. For each gold flower, work Pin Stitch with a floss Colonial Knot at center.

For each blue (square-shaped) flower, work Modified Loop Stitch, held down with a floss French Knot. Fill in remaining spaces with loose orchid and pink Colonial Knots.

Narcissus Basket

(see photo, front cover)

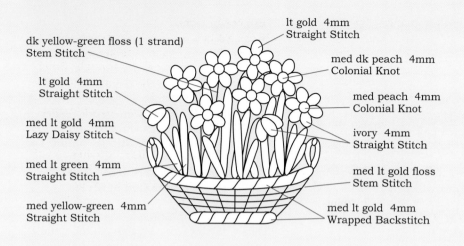

lt gold 4mm
Straight Stitch

dk yellow-green floss (1 strand)
Stem Stitch

med dk peach 4mm
Colonial Knot

lt gold 4mm
Straight Stitch

med peach 4mm
Colonial Knot

med lt gold 4mm
Lazy Daisy Stitch

ivory 4mm
Straight Stitch

med lt green 4mm
Straight Stitch

med lt gold floss
Stem Stitch

med yellow-green 4mm
Straight Stitch

med lt gold 4mm
Wrapped Backstitch

Stitching order:
Use floss to Stem Stitch open weave of basket. Work Wrapped Backstitch for base and rim and Lazy Daisy Stitches for handles.

Use floss to Stem Stitch stems. Work Straight Stitch leaves. For each narcissus, work Straight Stitch petals. Add a loose Colonial Knot at center of each full flower.

Ocean Floor

(see photo, page 17)

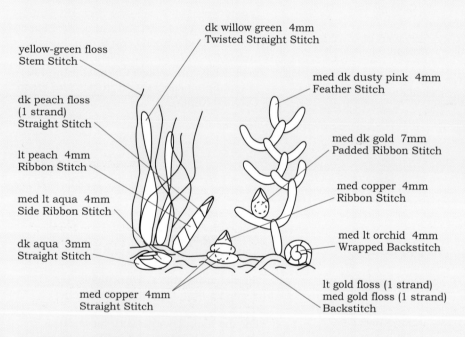

dk willow green 4mm
Twisted Straight Stitch

yellow-green floss
Stem Stitch

med dk dusty pink 4mm
Feather Stitch

dk peach floss
(1 strand)
Straight Stitch

med dk gold 7mm
Padded Ribbon Stitch

lt peach 4mm
Ribbon Stitch

med lt aqua 4mm
Side Ribbon Stitch

med copper 4mm
Ribbon Stitch

dk aqua 3mm
Straight Stitch

med lt orchid 4mm
Wrapped Backstitch

med copper 4mm
Straight Stitch

lt gold floss (1 strand)
med gold floss (1 strand)
Backstitch

Stitching order:
Work Twisted Straight Stitch plants and Feather Stitch coral.

Working creatures from left to right, for the first one, work one Straight Stitch covered by two Side Ribbon Stitches. For the second one, work a Ribbon Stitch; use floss to add Straight Stitches. For the third one, work a vertical Ribbon Stitch with the lower half (shown by dotted line) covered with two Straight Stitches.

For the fourth creature, work a Padded Ribbon Stitch (Ribbon Stitch over Colonial Knot). For the fifth creature, work Wrapped Backstitch in a circular shape.

Use floss to Stem Stitch wavy grass and blended floss to Backstitch sand.

Oriental Wisteria

(see photo, page 18)

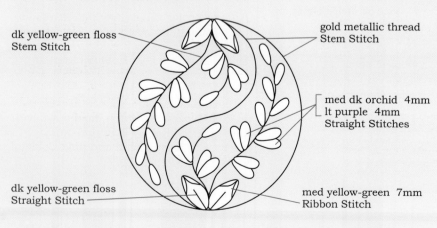

dk yellow-green floss
Stem Stitch

gold metallic thread
Stem Stitch

med dk orchid 4mm
lt purple 4mm
Straight Stitches

dk yellow-green floss
Straight Stitch

med yellow-green 7mm
Ribbon Stitch

Stitching order:
Use metallic thread to Stem Stitch outline and dividing line. Use floss to Stem Stitch stems. Work Ribbon Stitch leaves and work Straight Stitch blossoms in a random color arrangement.

Use floss to Straight Stitch a midrib on each leaf.

Pansy Wreath

(see photo, page 19)

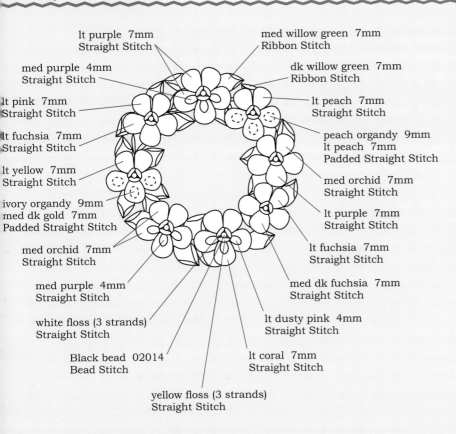

lt purple 7mm
Straight Stitch

med willow green 7mm
Ribbon Stitch

med purple 4mm
Straight Stitch

dk willow green 7mm
Ribbon Stitch

lt pink 7mm
Straight Stitch

lt peach 7mm
Straight Stitch

lt fuchsia 7mm
Straight Stitch

peach organdy 9mm
lt peach 7mm
Padded Straight Stitch

lt yellow 7mm
Straight Stitch

med orchid 7mm
Straight Stitch

ivory organdy 9mm
med dk gold 7mm
Padded Straight Stitch

lt purple 7mm
Straight Stitch

med orchid 7mm
Straight Stitch

med purple 4mm
Straight Stitch

lt fuchsia 7mm
Straight Stitch

med dk fuchsia 7mm
Straight Stitch

white floss (3 strands)
Straight Stitch

lt dusty pink 4mm
Straight Stitch

Black bead 02014
Bead Stitch

lt coral 7mm
Straight Stitch

yellow floss (3 strands)
Straight Stitch

Stitching order:

Work Ribbon Stitch leaves in two color values. Loosely work each pansy petal in one of the following ways: Straight Stitch, Padded Straight Stitch (organdy Straight Stitch over silk Straight Stitch), or a short Straight Stitch on top of a long Straight Stitch.

Use floss to work Straight Stitches to form a triangle at center of each pansy. Attach a seed bead at each center.

Parade of Plants

(see photo, back cover)

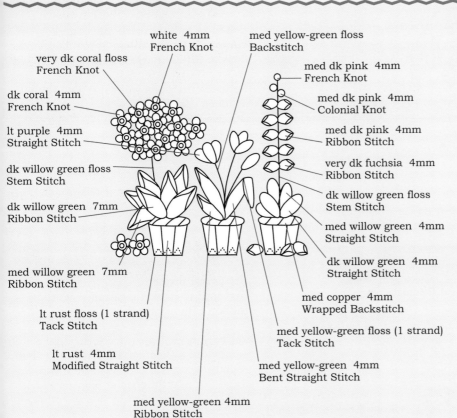

white 4mm
French Knot

med yellow-green floss
Backstitch

very dk coral floss
French Knot

med dk pink 4mm
French Knot

dk coral 4mm
French Knot

med dk pink 4mm
Colonial Knot

lt purple 4mm
Straight Stitch

med dk pink 4mm
Ribbon Stitch

dk willow green floss
Stem Stitch

very dk fuchsia 4mm
Ribbon Stitch

dk willow green 7mm
Ribbon Stitch

dk willow green floss
Stem Stitch

med willow green 4mm
Straight Stitch

med willow green 7mm
Ribbon Stitch

dk willow green 4mm
Straight Stitch

lt rust floss (1 strand)
Tack Stitch

med copper 4mm
Wrapped Backstitch

lt rust 4mm
Modified Straight Stitch

med yellow-green floss (1 strand)
Tack Stitch

med yellow-green 4mm
Bent Straight Stitch

med yellow-green 4mm
Ribbon Stitch

Stitching order:

For each flower pot, work three Modified Straight Stitches; tack edges in place. Work Wrapped Backstitch for rim.

Use floss to Stem Stitch or Backstitch stems. Work Ribbon Stitch and Straight Stitch leaves.

For coral flowers, work French Knot petals. At each center, work a ribbon French Knot with a floss French Knot on top. Work fallen flowers at base of pot.

For purple flowers, work overlapping Straight Stitches.

For fuchsia flowers, work Ribbon Stitch blossoms in two color values, then work Colonial Knots and a French Knot on top. Work fallen petals at base of pot.

Peony

(see photo, page 17)

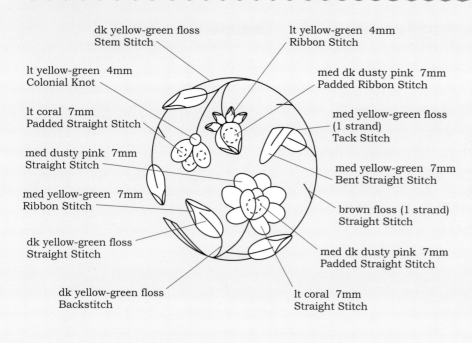

dk yellow-green floss
Stem Stitch

lt yellow-green 4mm
Ribbon Stitch

lt yellow-green 4mm
Colonial Knot

med dk dusty pink 7mm
Padded Ribbon Stitch

lt coral 7mm
Padded Straight Stitch

med yellow-green floss
(1 strand)
Tack Stitch

med dusty pink 7mm
Straight Stitch

med yellow-green 7mm
Bent Straight Stitch

med yellow-green 7mm
Ribbon Stitch

brown floss (1 strand)
Straight Stitch

dk yellow-green floss
Straight Stitch

med dk dusty pink 7mm
Padded Straight Stitch

dk yellow-green floss
Backstitch

lt coral 7mm
Straight Stitch

Stitching order:

Use floss to Stem Stitch main stem and Backstitch leaf stems; add side buds between leaves. Work one Bent Straight Stitch and the remaining Ribbon Stitch leaves. Use floss to Straight Stitch midribs on leaves.

For three-lobed bud, work three overlapping Padded Straight Stitches (Straight Stitch over Colonial Knot). Add a loose Colonial Knot at base.

For the tight bud, work Padded Ribbon Stitch (two Ribbon Stitches over one Colonial Knot) and Ribbon Stitches for calyx.

For the open flower, work Straight Stitches for the outside petals and Padded Straight Stitch (three Straight Stitches over one Colonial Knot) for center.

Pink Bellflower

(see photo, back cover)

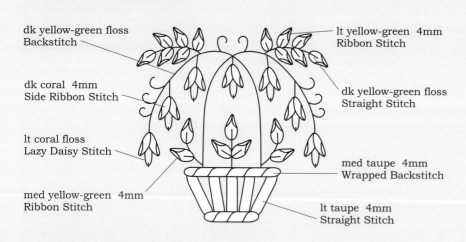

dk yellow-green floss
Backstitch

lt yellow-green 4mm
Ribbon Stitch

dk coral 4mm
Side Ribbon Stitch

dk yellow-green floss
Straight Stitch

lt coral floss
Lazy Daisy Stitch

med yellow-green 4mm
Ribbon Stitch

med taupe 4mm
Wrapped Backstitch

lt taupe 4mm
Straight Stitch

Stitching order:

Work basket with Straight Stitch sides and Wrapped Backstitch for rim and base.

Use floss to Backstitch stems and curliques. Work Ribbon Stitch leaves; use floss to Straight Stitch midribs.

For each blossom, work two Side Ribbon Stitches. Use floss to work a Lazy Daisy Stitch at center.

Potato Vine

(see photo, back cover)

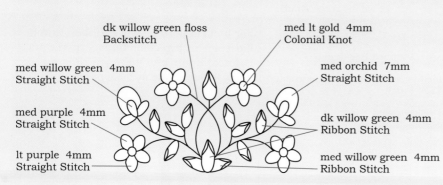

dk willow green floss
Backstitch

med lt gold 4mm
Colonial Knot

med willow green 4mm
Straight Stitch

med orchid 7mm
Straight Stitch

med purple 4mm
Straight Stitch

dk willow green 4mm
Ribbon Stitch

lt purple 4mm
Straight Stitch

med willow green 4mm
Ribbon Stitch

Stitching order:

Use floss to Backstitch stems. Work Ribbon Stitch leaves.

For each open flower, work Straight Stitch petals and a Colonial Knot at center. For each bud, work a Straight Stitch with three Straight Stitches at base for calyx.

Pumpkin Basket

(see photo, page 20)

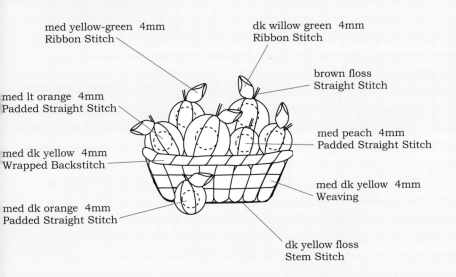

med yellow-green 4mm
Ribbon Stitch

dk willow green 4mm
Ribbon Stitch

brown floss
Straight Stitch

med lt orange 4mm
Padded Straight Stitch

med peach 4mm
Padded Straight Stitch

med dk yellow 4mm
Wrapped Backstitch

med dk yellow 4mm
Weaving

med dk orange 4mm
Padded Straight Stitch

dk yellow floss
Stem Stitch

Stitching order:

For basket, work short vertical stitches, then Weave with long horizontal stitches. Work Wrapped Backstitch for rim. Use floss to Stem Stitch sides and lower edge.

Work Padded Straight Stitch (three Straight Stitches over one Colonial Knot) for each pumpkin. Work Ribbon Stitch leaves. Use floss to work Straight Stitch stems.

Pumpkin Patch

(see photo, page 20)

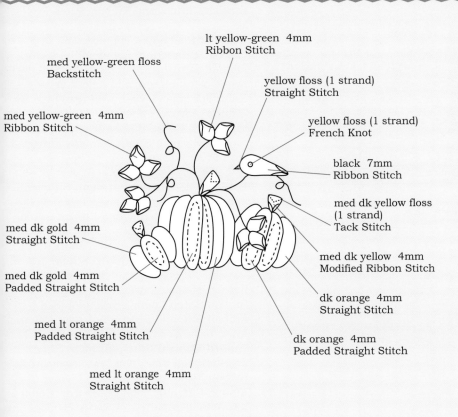

med yellow-green floss
Backstitch

lt yellow-green 4mm
Ribbon Stitch

yellow floss (1 strand)
Straight Stitch

med yellow-green 4mm
Ribbon Stitch

yellow floss (1 strand)
French Knot

black 7mm
Ribbon Stitch

med dk yellow floss
(1 strand)
Tack Stitch

med dk gold 4mm
Straight Stitch

med dk yellow 4mm
Modified Ribbon Stitch

med dk gold 4mm
Padded Straight Stitch

dk orange 4mm
Straight Stitch

med lt orange 4mm
Padded Straight Stitch

dk orange 4mm
Padded Straight Stitch

med lt orange 4mm
Straight Stitch

Stitching order:

Work pumpkins from right to left. For the first two, work Straight Stitches with the middle two being Padded Straight Stitch (Straight Stitch over Straight Stitch). For the smallest pumpkin, work two side Straight Stitches and a Padded Straight Stitch (Straight Stitch over Straight Stitch) at center. Work Modified Ribbon Stitch stems.

Use floss to Backstitch stems and tendrils. Work Ribbon Stitch leaves.

For the crow, work a Ribbon Stitch body. Use floss to make a French Knot eye and Straight Stitch beak.

Rambling Rose

(see photo, page 17)

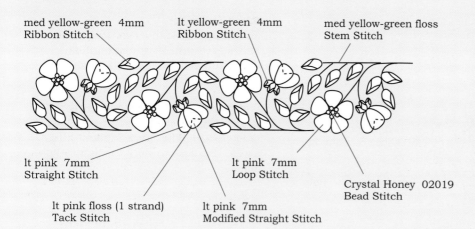

med yellow-green 4mm
Ribbon Stitch

lt yellow-green 4mm
Ribbon Stitch

med yellow-green floss
Stem Stitch

lt pink 7mm
Straight Stitch

lt pink 7mm
Loop Stitch

Crystal Honey 02019
Bead Stitch

lt pink floss (1 strand)
Tack Stitch

lt pink 7mm
Modified Straight Stitch

Stitching order:
Use floss to Stem Stitch stems. Work Ribbon Stitch leaves.

For full flowers, work Loop Stitch petals. Attach a group of beads at center. For partial flowers, work Straight Stitch side petals and a Modified Straight Stitch centered on top. Add Ribbon Stitches for calyx.

Note: This design can be repeated to form a continuous border.

Rhapsody in Blue

(see photo, back cover)

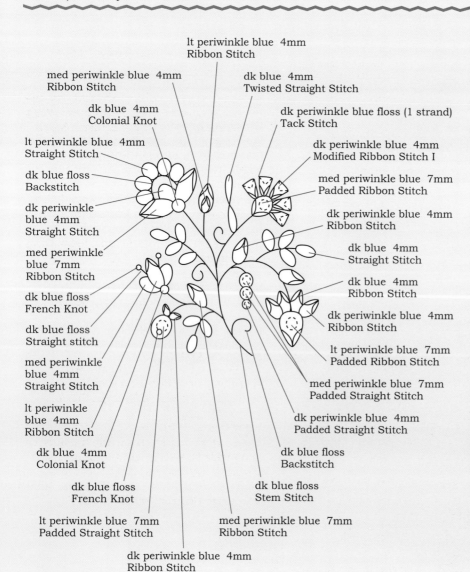

lt periwinkle blue 4mm
Ribbon Stitch

med periwinkle blue 4mm
Ribbon Stitch

dk blue 4mm
Twisted Straight Stitch

dk blue 4mm
Colonial Knot

dk periwinkle blue floss (1 strand)
Tack Stitch

lt periwinkle blue 4mm
Straight Stitch

dk periwinkle blue 4mm
Modified Ribbon Stitch I

dk blue floss
Backstitch

med periwinkle blue 7mm
Padded Ribbon Stitch

dk periwinkle
blue 4mm
Straight Stitch

dk periwinkle blue 4mm
Ribbon Stitch

med periwinkle
blue 7mm
Ribbon Stitch

dk blue 4mm
Straight Stitch

dk blue floss
French Knot

dk blue 4mm
Ribbon Stitch

dk blue floss
Straight stitch

dk periwinkle blue 4mm
Ribbon Stitch

med periwinkle
blue 4mm
Straight Stitch

lt periwinkle blue 7mm
Padded Ribbon Stitch

lt periwinkle
blue 4mm
Ribbon Stitch

med periwinkle blue 7mm
Padded Straight Stitch

dk blue 4mm
Colonial Knot

dk periwinkle blue 4mm
Padded Straight Stitch

dk blue floss
French Knot

dk blue floss
Backstitch

lt periwinkle blue 7mm
Padded Straight Stitch

dk blue floss
Stem Stitch

med periwinkle blue 7mm
Ribbon Stitch

dk periwinkle blue 4mm
Ribbon Stitch

Stitching order:
Use floss to Stem Stitch stems and Backstitch curliques and outline on top left flower. Work Straight Stitch, Twisted Straight Stitch, and Ribbon Stitch leaves.

Begin at the bottom left and work in a clockwise direction. For small bud, work a Padded Straight Stitch (Straight Stitch over Colonial Knot); add a floss French Knot. For small flower, work two Straight Stitches with a Ribbon Stitch centered on top. Add a Colonial Knot at base. Use floss to work Straight Stitch stamens topped with French Knots.

For large flower, work Straight Stitches above floss outline. Below outline, work one Straight Stitch with a Ribbon Stitch on each side and a loose Colonial Knot at base. For small bud, work a short Ribbon Stitch over a longer Ribbon Stitch.

For fan-shaped flower, work Modified Ribbon Stitch I petals with a Padded Ribbon Stitch (Ribbon Stitch over Colonial Knot) base. For triple berry flower, work Padded Straight Stitch (Straight Stitch over Colonial Knot). For last flower, work Ribbon Stitch petals above a Padded Ribbon Stitch (Ribbon Stitch over Colonial Knot).

Roly-Poly Santa

(see photo, page 20)

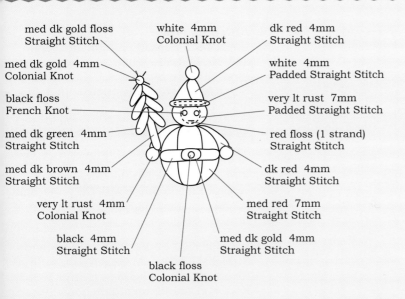

med dk gold floss
Straight Stitch

white 4mm
Colonial Knot

dk red 4mm
Straight Stitch

med dk gold 4mm
Colonial Knot

white 4mm
Padded Straight Stitch

black floss
French Knot

very lt rust 7mm
Padded Straight Stitch

med dk green 4mm
Straight Stitch

red floss (1 strand)
Straight Stitch

med dk brown 4mm
Straight Stitch

dk red 4mm
Straight Stitch

very lt rust 4mm
Colonial Knot

med red 7mm
Straight Stitch

black 4mm
Straight Stitch

med dk gold 4mm
Straight Stitch

black floss
Colonial Knot

Stitching order:

Work Straight Stitches for body, belt, and buckle; anchor buckle with a floss Colonial Knot.

Work Straight Stitch arms and a Padded Straight Stitch (Straight Stitch over Colonial Knot) head. Use floss to work French Knot eyes and a Straight Stitch mouth. Work two Straight Stitches for hat topped with a loose Colonial Knot. Add a Padded Straight Stitch (Straight Stitch over Straight Stitch) brim.

Work Straight Stitches for the tree trunk and branches. Work Colonial Knots for hands and star center. Use floss to work Straight Stitch rays from star center.

Rose Border

(see photo, page 18)

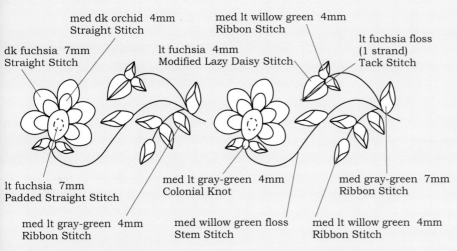

med dk orchid 4mm
Straight Stitch

med lt willow green 4mm
Ribbon Stitch

dk fuchsia 7mm
Straight Stitch

lt fuchsia 4mm
Modified Lazy Daisy Stitch

lt fuchsia floss
(1 strand)
Tack Stitch

lt fuchsia 7mm
Padded Straight Stitch

med lt gray-green 4mm
Colonial Knot

med gray-green 7mm
Ribbon Stitch

med lt gray-green 4mm
Ribbon Stitch

med willow green floss
Stem Stitch

med lt willow green 4mm
Ribbon Stitch

Stitching order:

Use floss to Stem Stitch stems. Work Ribbon Stitch leaves.

For the flower, work long Straight Stitches topped by shorter Straight Stitches. Work a Padded Straight Stitch (Straight Stitch over Colonial Knot) at center. Work two Ribbon Stitches and a Colonial Knot for calyx.

For the bud, work a Modified Lazy Daisy Stitch and two Ribbon Stitches for calyx.

Note: This design can be repeated to form a continuous border.

Roses Are Roses

(see photo, front cover)

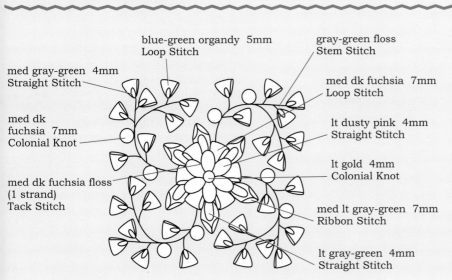

blue-green organdy 5mm
Loop Stitch

gray-green floss
Stem Stitch

med gray-green 4mm
Straight Stitch

med dk fuchsia 7mm
Loop Stitch

med dk
fuchsia 7mm
Colonial Knot

lt dusty pink 4mm
Straight Stitch

lt gold 4mm
Colonial Knot

med dk fuchsia floss
(1 strand)
Tack Stitch

med lt gray-green 7mm
Ribbon Stitch

lt gray-green 4mm
Straight Stitch

Stitching order:

Use floss to Stem Stitch stems. Work organdy Loop Stitch leaves, each anchored at base with a Straight Stitch.

Work Colonial Knot buds. For center flower, work outside Loop Stitch petals and inside loose Straight Stitch petals. Work a loose Colonial Knot at center. Between petals, work short Straight Stitch over longer Ribbon Stitch leaves.

School of Fish

(see photo, page 17)

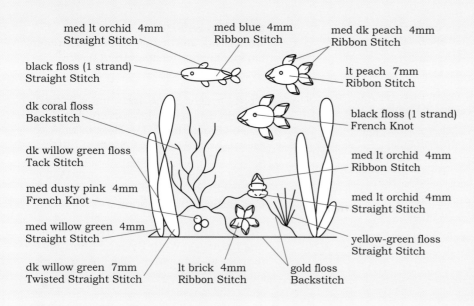

med lt orchid 4mm
Straight Stitch

med blue 4mm
Ribbon Stitch

med dk peach 4mm
Ribbon Stitch

black floss (1 strand)
Straight Stitch

lt peach 7mm
Ribbon Stitch

dk coral floss
Backstitch

black floss (1 strand)
French Knot

dk willow green floss
Tack Stitch

med lt orchid 4mm
Ribbon Stitch

med dusty pink 4mm
French Knot

med lt orchid 4mm
Straight Stitch

med willow green 4mm
Straight Stitch

yellow-green floss
Straight Stitch

dk willow green 7mm
Twisted Straight Stitch

lt brick 4mm
Ribbon Stitch

gold floss
Backstitch

Stitching order:

Use floss to Backstitch coral and sand and Straight Stitch narrow green leaves. Work Straight Stitch and Twisted Straight Stitch leaves; tack the twisted stitch to expose coral.

Work the sea creatures from left to right. For the first sea creature, work three French Knots. For the second, work five Ribbon Stitches. For the third, work a vertical Ribbon Stitch with the lower half (shown by dotted line) covered with two Straight Stitches.

For blue fish, work a Ribbon Stitch and Straight Stitches. For peach fish, work Ribbon Stitches. Use floss to work French Knot eyes and Straight Stitch mouths on each fish.

Seashell Collection

(see photo, page 17)

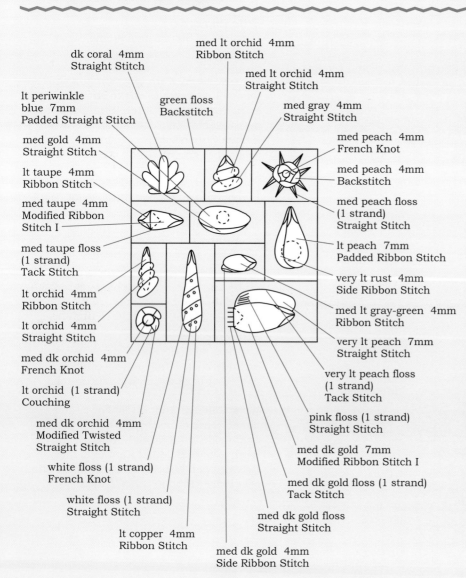

dk coral 4mm
Straight Stitch

med lt orchid 4mm
Ribbon Stitch

med lt orchid 4mm
Straight Stitch

lt periwinkle
blue 7mm
Padded Straight Stitch

green floss
Backstitch

med gray 4mm
Straight Stitch

med peach 4mm
French Knot

med gold 4mm
Straight Stitch

med peach 4mm
Backstitch

lt taupe 4mm
Ribbon Stitch

med peach floss
(1 strand)
Straight Stitch

med taupe 4mm
Modified Ribbon
Stitch I

med taupe floss
(1 strand)
Tack Stitch

lt peach 7mm
Padded Ribbon Stitch

lt orchid 4mm
Ribbon Stitch

very lt rust 4mm
Side Ribbon Stitch

lt orchid 4mm
Straight Stitch

med lt gray-green 4mm
Ribbon Stitch

med dk orchid 4mm
French Knot

very lt peach 7mm
Straight Stitch

lt orchid (1 strand)
Couching

very lt peach floss
(1 strand)
Tack Stitch

med dk orchid 4mm
Modified Twisted
Straight Stitch

pink floss (1 strand)
Straight Stitch

white floss (1 strand)
French Knot

med dk gold 7mm
Modified Ribbon Stitch I

white floss (1 strand)
Straight Stitch

med dk gold floss (1 strand)
Tack Stitch

lt copper 4mm
Ribbon Stitch

med dk gold floss
Straight Stitch

med dk gold 4mm
Side Ribbon Stitch

Stitching order:

Use floss to Backstitch outlines. Work the shells from left to right and from the top down. For first shell, work overlapping Straight Stitches. For second shell, work a Ribbon Stitch with lower half (shown by dotted lines) covered by two Straight Stitches. For third shell, work a French Knot surrounded by Backstitch; use floss to Straight Stitch rays.

For second row, work the first shell with a Ribbon Stitch covered with a Modified Ribbon Stitch I. Work second shell with a Straight Stitch partially covered by a Padded Straight Stitch (Straight Stitch over French Knot). For third (vertical) shell, work a Side Ribbon Stitch partially covered by a Padded Ribbon Stitch (Ribbon Stitch over Colonial Knot).

For last row, work first shell with a Ribbon Stitch with lower half (shown by dotted lines) covered by diagonal Straight Stitches. Work shell below it with a French Knot center, surrounded by a Modified Twisted Straight Stitch. Couch coil with floss. Work next shell with a Ribbon Stitch; add floss Straight Stitches and French Knots. Work small green shell with a Side Ribbon Stitch almost covered by a loose Ribbon Stitch. For last shell, work a Straight Stitch partially covered by a Modified Ribbon Stitch I, each tacked to create shape. Add floss Straight Stitches.

Secret Place I

(see photo, page 19)

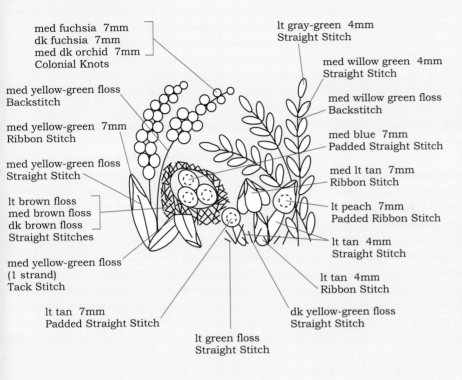

med fuchsia 7mm
dk fuchsia 7mm
med dk orchid 7mm
Colonial Knots

med yellow-green floss
Backstitch

med yellow-green 7mm
Ribbon Stitch

med yellow-green floss
Straight Stitch

lt brown floss
med brown floss
dk brown floss
Straight Stitches

med yellow-green floss
(1 strand)
Tack Stitch

lt tan 7mm
Padded Straight Stitch

lt green floss
Straight Stitch

lt gray-green 4mm
Straight Stitch

med willow green 4mm
Straight Stitch

med willow green floss
Backstitch

med blue 7mm
Padded Straight Stitch

med lt tan 7mm
Ribbon Stitch

lt peach 7mm
Padded Ribbon Stitch

lt tan 4mm
Straight Stitch

lt tan 4mm
Ribbon Stitch

dk yellow-green floss
Straight Stitch

Stitching order:

Use floss to Backstitch stems; use three color values in a random arrangement to Straight Stitch nest.

Work small Straight Stitch leaves. Work Straight Stitch and Ribbon Stitch mushroom stems. Work large Ribbon Stitch leaves, tacking one as for Bent Straight Stitch. Add floss Straight Stitch midribs on leaves.

For fuchsia flowers, work Colonial Knots in a random color arrangement using three color values. For the eggs and the first mushroom, work Padded Straight Stitch (Straight Stitch over Colonial Knot). For remaining mushrooms, work overlapping Ribbon Stitch and Padded Ribbon Stitch (Ribbon Stitch over Colonial Knot).

Use two color values of floss to Straight Stitch grass in front of mushrooms.

Secret Place II

(see photo, back cover)

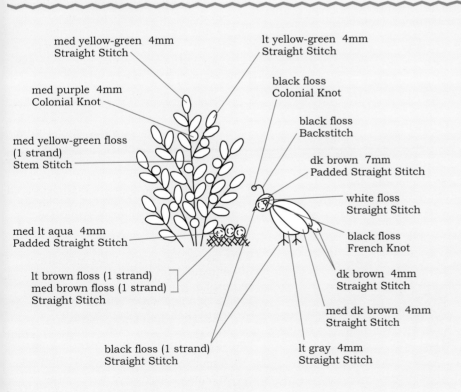

med yellow-green 4mm
Straight Stitch

med purple 4mm
Colonial Knot

med yellow-green floss
(1 strand)
Stem Stitch

med lt aqua 4mm
Padded Straight Stitch

lt brown floss (1 strand)
med brown floss (1 strand)
Straight Stitch

black floss (1 strand)
Straight Stitch

lt yellow-green 4mm
Straight Stitch

black floss
Colonial Knot

black floss
Backstitch

dk brown 7mm
Padded Straight Stitch

white floss
Straight Stitch

black floss
French Knot

dk brown 4mm
Straight Stitch

med dk brown 4mm
Straight Stitch

lt gray 4mm
Straight Stitch

Stitching order:

Use floss to Stem Stitch stems; Straight Stitch nest with blended floss.

Work Straight Stitch leaves and Colonial Knot berries. For eggs, work Padded Straight Stitch (Straight Stitch over French Knot).

For bird, work Straight Stitch tail, body, and wings and a Padded Straight Stitch (Straight Stitch over Colonial Knot) for head. Use floss to Straight Stitch head markings, beak, and feet; work Backstitch and a Colonial Knot for head curlique and a French Knot eye.

Sewing Whatnots

(see photo, page 20)

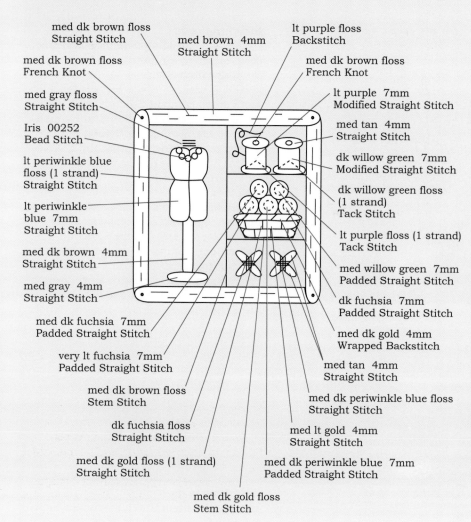

med dk brown floss
Straight Stitch

med dk brown floss
French Knot

med gray floss
Straight Stitch

Iris 00252
Bead Stitch

lt periwinkle blue
floss (1 strand)
Straight Stitch

lt periwinkle
blue 7mm
Straight Stitch

med dk brown 4mm
Straight Stitch

med gray 4mm
Straight Stitch

med dk fuchsia 7mm
Padded Straight Stitch

very lt fuchsia 7mm
Padded Straight Stitch

med dk brown floss
Stem Stitch

dk fuchsia floss
Straight Stitch

med dk gold floss (1 strand)
Straight Stitch

med brown 4mm
Straight Stitch

lt purple floss
Backstitch

med dk brown floss
French Knot

lt purple 7mm
Modified Straight Stitch

med tan 4mm
Straight Stitch

dk willow green 7mm
Modified Straight Stitch

dk willow green floss
(1 strand)
Tack Stitch

lt purple floss (1 strand)
Tack Stitch

med willow green 7mm
Padded Straight Stitch

dk fuchsia 7mm
Padded Straight Stitch

med dk gold 4mm
Wrapped Backstitch

med tan 4mm
Straight Stitch

med dk periwinkle blue floss
Straight Stitch

med lt gold 4mm
Straight Stitch

med dk periwinkle blue 7mm
Padded Straight Stitch

med dk gold floss
Stem Stitch

Stitching order:

Use floss to Stem Stitch separating outlines. For the dressmaker's form, work Straight Stitches for base. Work two vertical Straight Stitches for body; work floss Straight Stitch to create shape. Use floss to Straight Stitch neck and attach seed beads arranged as a necklace.

Work Modified Straight Stitch for each spool of thread. Work Straight Stitches for top and bottom of each spool. Use floss to Backstitch loose thread and add a French Knot to top of each spool.

For the basket, work a Straight Stitch side and Wrapped Backstitch rim. Use floss to Stem Stitch sides and bottom and Straight Stitch weaving lines. Work a Padded Straight Stitch (Straight Stitch over Colonial Knot) for each yarn ball.

Work Straight Stitches that cross each other for bobbins. Use floss to Straight Stitch yarn on bobbins.

For the frame, work long Straight Stitches; use floss to anchor each side with random Straight Stitches, adding a French Knot at each corner.

Spring Wreath

(see photo, back cover)

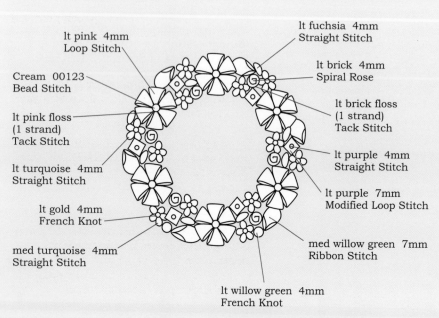

lt pink 4mm
Loop Stitch

Cream 00123
Bead Stitch

lt pink floss
(1 strand)
Tack Stitch

lt turquoise 4mm
Straight Stitch

lt gold 4mm
French Knot

med turquoise 4mm
Straight Stitch

lt fuchsia 4mm
Straight Stitch

lt brick 4mm
Spiral Rose

lt brick floss
(1 strand)
Tack Stitch

lt purple 4mm
Straight Stitch

lt purple 7mm
Modified Loop Stitch

med willow green 7mm
Ribbon Stitch

lt willow green 4mm
French Knot

Stitching order:

Work pink Loop Stitch flowers, adding a seed bead at each center. Work Ribbon Stitch leaves.

Work turquoise flowers with Straight Stitch petals and a French Knot at each center. For purple flowers, work Modified Loop Stitch held down with a small Straight Stitch.

For fuchsia buds, work Straight Stitches. For each brick flower, work a spiral Rose.

Note: If desired, fill in any spaces with lt willow green 4mm French Knots.

Springtime Heart

(see photo, front cover)

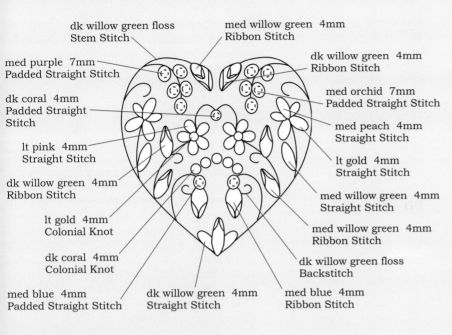

dk willow green floss
Stem Stitch

med willow green 4mm
Ribbon Stitch

dk willow green 4mm
Ribbon Stitch

med purple 7mm
Padded Straight Stitch

dk coral 4mm
Padded Straight
Stitch

med orchid 7mm
Padded Straight Stitch

lt pink 4mm
Straight Stitch

med peach 4mm
Straight Stitch

dk willow green 4mm
Ribbon Stitch

lt gold 4mm
Straight Stitch

lt gold 4mm
Colonial Knot

med willow green 4mm
Straight Stitch

dk coral 4mm
Colonial Knot

med willow green 4mm
Ribbon Stitch

med blue 4mm
Padded Straight Stitch

dk willow green floss
Backstitch

dk willow green 4mm
Straight Stitch

med blue 4mm
Ribbon Stitch

Stitching order:
Use floss to Stem Stitch outline and stems and Backstitch curliques. Work Straight Stitch and Ribbon Stitch leaves; the center top leaves each have a short Ribbon Stitch over a longer Ribbon Stitch.

For grapes, work Padded Straight Stitch (Straight Stitch over Colonial Knot). For coral berries, work Colonial Knots.

For peach/gold flowers and pink flowers, work Straight Stitch petals. Add a Colonial Knot to center of each pink flower. For each blue blossom, work a Ribbon Stitch topped with a Padded Straight Stitch (Straight Stitch over Colonial Knot). For center bud between pink flowers, work a Padded Straight Stitch (Straight Stitch over Colonial Knot).

Strawberry Roundel

(see photo, page 17)

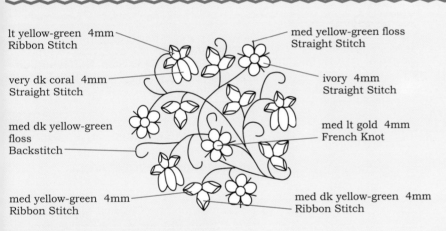

lt yellow-green 4mm
Ribbon Stitch

med yellow-green floss
Straight Stitch

very dk coral 4mm
Straight Stitch

ivory 4mm
Straight Stitch

med dk yellow-green
floss
Backstitch

med lt gold 4mm
French Knot

med yellow-green 4mm
Ribbon Stitch

med dk yellow-green 4mm
Ribbon Stitch

Stitching order:
Use floss to Backstitch stems and curliques. Work Ribbon Stitch leaves using two color values on each triple leaf.

For each strawberry, work three Straight Stitches with three Ribbon Stitches for the calyx.

For the blossoms, work loose Straight Stitch petals and a French Knot at center. Use floss to work Straight Stitches between petals.

Sunflower Sampling

(see photo, page 20)

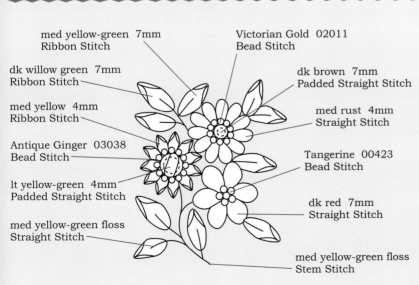

med yellow-green 7mm
Ribbon Stitch

Victorian Gold 02011
Bead Stitch

dk willow green 7mm
Ribbon Stitch

dk brown 7mm
Padded Straight Stitch

med yellow 4mm
Ribbon Stitch

med rust 4mm
Straight Stitch

Antique Ginger 03038
Bead Stitch

Tangerine 00423
Bead Stitch

lt yellow-green 4mm
Padded Straight Stitch

med yellow-green floss
Straight Stitch

dk red 7mm
Straight Stitch

med yellow-green floss
Stem Stitch

Stitching order:
Use floss to Stem Stitch stems. Work Ribbon Stitch leaves; add a floss Straight Stitch midrib to each leaf.

For the yellow flower, work Ribbon Stitch petals with a Padded Straight Stitch (three Straight Stitches over one Colonial Knot) center. Attach beads around center.

For the rust (middle) flower, work Straight Stitch petals with a Padded Straight Stitch (Straight Stitch over a Colonial Knot) center. Attach beads around center. For the red flower, work Straight Stitch petals. Attach a group of beads at center.

Symphony of Roses I

(see photo, front cover)

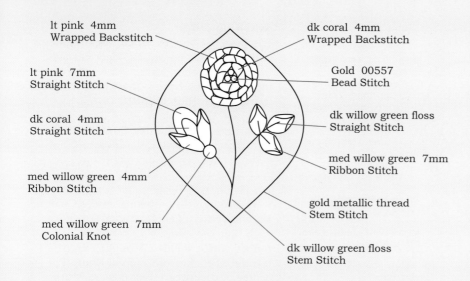

lt pink 4mm
Wrapped Backstitch

lt pink 7mm
Straight Stitch

dk coral 4mm
Straight Stitch

med willow green 4mm
Ribbon Stitch

med willow green 7mm
Colonial Knot

dk coral 4mm
Wrapped Backstitch

Gold 00557
Bead Stitch

dk willow green floss
Straight Stitch

med willow green 7mm
Ribbon Stitch

gold metallic thread
Stem Stitch

dk willow green floss
Stem Stitch

Note: The Symphony of Roses designs I through V can form a horizontal border of adjacent designs or a vertical border with the points touching; the vertical border can also be worked along a curve.

Stitching order:
Use metallic thread to Stem Stitch outline. Use floss to Stem Stitch stems.

For main flower leave a space at center, then work three rows of Wrapped Backstitch; work two inside rows in dark value, outer row in a light value. Add three seed beads at center.

For bud, work a short Straight Stitch over a longer Straight Stitch. Work Ribbon Stitch leaves. Add a Colonial Knot at base of bud. On leaf spray at right, use floss to Straight Stitch midribs of leaves.

Symphony of Roses II

(see photo, page 18)

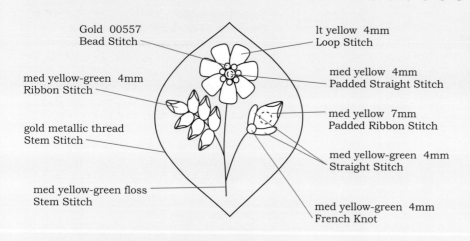

Gold 00557
Bead Stitch

med yellow-green 4mm
Ribbon Stitch

gold metallic thread
Stem Stitch

med yellow-green floss
Stem Stitch

lt yellow 4mm
Loop Stitch

med yellow 4mm
Padded Straight Stitch

med yellow 7mm
Padded Ribbon Stitch

med yellow-green 4mm
Straight Stitch

med yellow-green 4mm
French Knot

Stitching order:
Use metallic thread to Stem Stitch outline. Use floss to Stem Stitch stems. Work Ribbon Stitch leaves.

For the flower, work Loop Stitch petals with a Padded Straight Stitch (Straight Stitch over Colonial Knot) center. Attach seed beads around center knot.

For the bud, work a Padded Ribbon Stitch (Ribbon Stitch over Colonial Knot). Add two Straight Stitches and a French Knot for calyx.

Symphony of Roses III

(see photo, page 18)

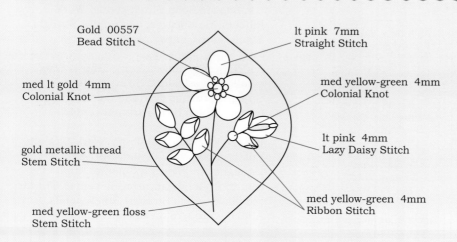

Gold 00557
Bead Stitch

med lt gold 4mm
Colonial Knot

gold metallic thread
Stem Stitch

med yellow-green floss
Stem Stitch

lt pink 7mm
Straight Stitch

med yellow-green 4mm
Colonial Knot

lt pink 4mm
Lazy Daisy Stitch

med yellow-green 4mm
Ribbon Stitch

Stitching order:
Use metallic thread to Stem Stitch outline. Use floss to Stem Stitch stems. Work Ribbon Stitch leaves.

For the flower, work very loose Straight Stitch petals with a loose Colonial Knot center. Attach seed beads around center knot.

For the bud, work a Lazy Daisy Stitch. Add Ribbon Stitches and a Colonial Knot for calyx.

Symphony of Roses IV

(see photo, page 18)

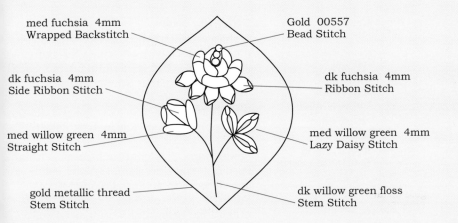

med fuchsia 4mm
Wrapped Backstitch

dk fuchsia 4mm
Side Ribbon Stitch

med willow green 4mm
Straight Stitch

gold metallic thread
Stem Stitch

Gold 00557
Bead Stitch

dk fuchsia 4mm
Ribbon Stitch

med willow green 4mm
Lazy Daisy Stitch

dk willow green floss
Stem Stitch

Stitching order:

Use metallic thread to Stem Stitch outline. Use floss to Stem Stitch stems. Work Lazy Daisy leaves.

For the bud, work two Side Ribbon Stitches. Add Straight Stitches for calyx.

For the flower, work Ribbon Stitches for the lower petals. Loosely work two rows of Wrapped Backstitch for center area, forming a "V" shape. Attach a row of three seed beads at center "V."

Symphony of Roses V

(see photo, page 18)

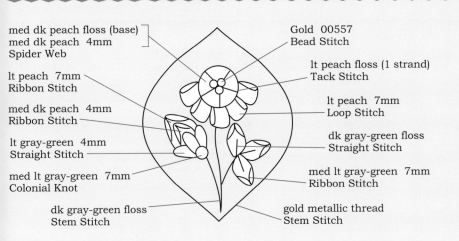

med dk peach floss (base)
med dk peach 4mm
Spider Web

lt peach 7mm
Ribbon Stitch

med dk peach 4mm
Ribbon Stitch

lt gray-green 4mm
Straight Stitch

med lt gray-green 7mm
Colonial Knot

dk gray-green floss
Stem Stitch

Gold 00557
Bead Stitch

lt peach floss (1 strand)
Tack Stitch

lt peach 7mm
Loop Stitch

dk gray-green floss
Straight Stitch

med lt gray-green 7mm
Ribbon Stitch

gold metallic thread
Stem Stitch

Stitching order:

Use metallic thread to Stem Stitch outline. Use floss to Stem Stitch stems. Work Ribbon Stitch leaves, adding a floss Straight Stitch midrib to each leaf.

For the bud, work a Ribbon Stitch then a shorter Ribbon Stitch on top. Work Straight Stitches for calyx and a Colonial Knot at base.

For the flower, work Loop Stitch petals. Work a Spider Web above petals. Attach three seed beads at Spider Web center.

Teacup Wreath

(see photo, back cover)

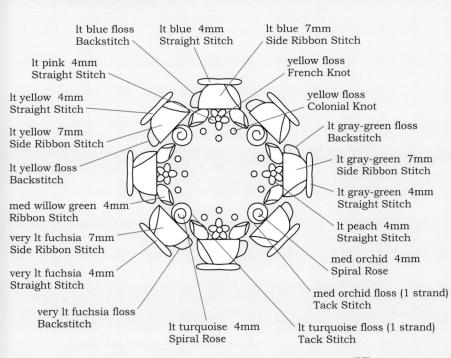

lt blue floss
Backstitch

lt pink 4mm
Straight Stitch

lt yellow 4mm
Straight Stitch

lt yellow 7mm
Side Ribbon Stitch

lt yellow floss
Backstitch

med willow green 4mm
Ribbon Stitch

very lt fuchsia 7mm
Side Ribbon Stitch

very lt fuchsia 4mm
Straight Stitch

very lt fuchsia floss
Backstitch

lt turquoise 4mm
Spiral Rose

lt blue 4mm
Straight Stitch

lt blue 7mm
Side Ribbon Stitch

yellow floss
French Knot

yellow floss
Colonial Knot

lt gray-green floss
Backstitch

lt gray-green 7mm
Side Ribbon Stitch

lt gray-green 4mm
Straight Stitch

lt peach 4mm
Straight Stitch

med orchid 4mm
Spiral Rose

med orchid floss (1 strand)
Tack Stitch

lt turquoise floss (1 strand)
Tack Stitch

Stitching order:

Work a Side Ribbon Stitch for each teacup; if needed, tack with matching floss to retain shape. Use floss to Backstitch each handle. Work a Straight Stitch for each saucer.

Work Ribbon Stitch leaves. For orchid and turquoise flowers, work Spiral Rose. For pink and peach flowers, work Straight Stitch petals; use floss to work a French Knot at center. Above each pink or peach flower, use floss to work three Colonial Knots.

Teacups on Parade

(see photo, back cover)

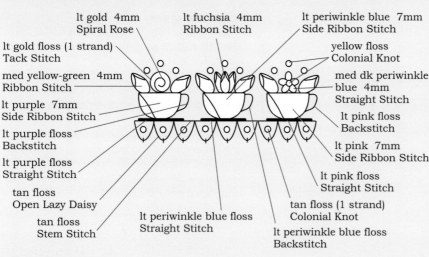

lt gold 4mm
Spiral Rose

lt fuchsia 4mm
Ribbon Stitch

lt periwinkle blue 7mm
Side Ribbon Stitch

yellow floss
Colonial Knot

lt gold floss (1 strand)
Tack Stitch

med yellow-green 4mm
Ribbon Stitch

med dk periwinkle
blue 4mm
Straight Stitch

lt purple 7mm
Side Ribbon Stitch

lt pink floss
Backstitch

lt purple floss
Backstitch

lt pink 7mm
Side Ribbon Stitch

lt purple floss
Straight Stitch

lt pink floss
Straight Stitch

tan floss
Open Lazy Daisy

tan floss
Stem Stitch

lt periwinkle blue floss
Straight Stitch

tan floss (1 strand)
Colonial Knot

lt periwinkle blue floss
Backstitch

Stitching order:

Work a Side Ribbon Stitch for each teacup; if needed, tack with matching floss to create shape. Use floss to Backstitch each handle and Straight Stitch each saucer.

Work Ribbon Stitch leaves. For gold flower, work a Spiral Rose. For fuchsia flower, work overlapping Ribbon Stitches. For blue flower, work Straight Stitch petals with a floss Colonial Knot center. Above each flower, work three floss Colonial Knots. For tablecloth, use floss to work a Stem Stitch line. Below line work a series of Open Lazy Daisy Stitches with a Colonial Knot centered in each.

Thistles

(see photo, page 19)

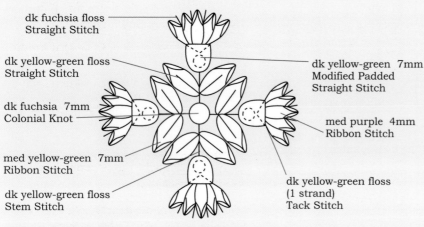

dk fuchsia floss
Straight Stitch

dk yellow-green floss
Straight Stitch

dk yellow-green 7mm
Modified Padded
Straight Stitch

dk fuchsia 7mm
Colonial Knot

med purple 4mm
Ribbon Stitch

med yellow-green 7mm
Ribbon Stitch

dk yellow-green floss
Stem Stitch

dk yellow-green floss
(1 strand)
Tack Stitch

Stitching order:

Use floss to Stem Stitch stems. Work Ribbon Stitch leaves. Use floss to work a Straight Stitch midrib on each leaf.

At base of each flower, work a Modified Padded Straight Stitch (Straight Stitch over Colonial Knot), tacking as needed to create shape. Work overlapping Ribbon Stitch petals. Use floss to work Straight Stitches between petals.

Work a loose Colonial Knot at center of design.

Tree of Life

(see photo, page 19)

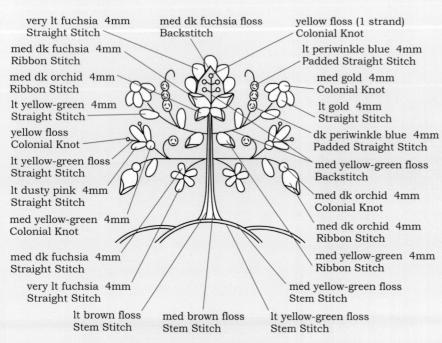

very lt fuchsia 4mm
Straight Stitch

med dk fuchsia floss
Backstitch

yellow floss (1 strand)
Colonial Knot

med dk fuchsia 4mm
Ribbon Stitch

lt periwinkle blue 4mm
Padded Straight Stitch

med dk orchid 4mm
Ribbon Stitch

med gold 4mm
Colonial Knot

lt yellow-green 4mm
Straight Stitch

lt gold 4mm
Straight Stitch

yellow floss
Colonial Knot

dk periwinkle blue 4mm
Padded Straight Stitch

lt yellow-green floss
Straight Stitch

med yellow-green floss
Backstitch

lt dusty pink 4mm
Straight Stitch

med dk orchid 4mm
Colonial Knot

med yellow-green 4mm
Colonial Knot

med dk orchid 4mm
Ribbon Stitch

med dk fuchsia 4mm
Straight Stitch

med yellow-green 4mm
Ribbon Stitch

very lt fuchsia 4mm
Straight Stitch

med yellow-green floss
Stem Stitch

lt brown floss
Stem Stitch

med brown floss
Stem Stitch

lt yellow-green floss
Stem Stitch

Stitching order:

Use two color values of floss to work Stem Stitch rows for ground; work Stem Stitch tree trunk. Backstitch branches and curliques with floss. Work Straight Stitch and Ribbon Stitch leaves. For center top flower, use floss to Backstitch arched outline and center stem; add Colonial Knots at stem ends. Work five Straight Stitches at top and overlapping Ribbon Stitches at base.

For blue buds, work Padded Straight Stitch (Straight Stitch over Colonial Knot). For each yellow blossom, work Straight Stitch petals and a Colonial Knot center. For pink flowers, work Straight Stitch petals with a Colonial Knot base. Straight Stitch floss stamens with Colonial Knot ends. For each orchid blossom, work a Ribbon Stitch with a Colonial Knot base. For fuchsia flowers, work Straight Stitch petals.

Trellis Garden

(see photo, page 18)

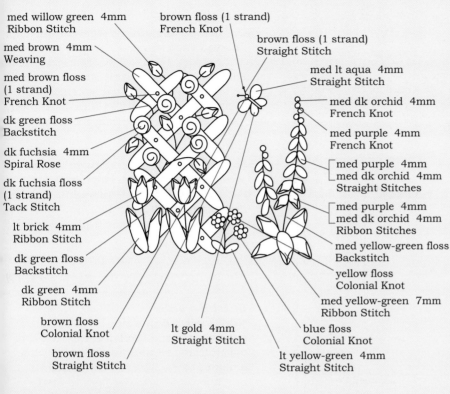

med willow green 4mm
Ribbon Stitch

med brown 4mm
Weaving

med brown floss
(1 strand)
French Knot

dk green floss
Backstitch

dk fuchsia 4mm
Spiral Rose

dk fuchsia floss
(1 strand)
Tack Stitch

lt brick 4mm
Ribbon Stitch

dk green floss
Backstitch

dk green 4mm
Ribbon Stitch

brown floss
Colonial Knot

brown floss
Straight Stitch

brown floss (1 strand)
French Knot

brown floss (1 strand)
Straight Stitch

med lt aqua 4mm
Straight Stitch

med dk orchid 4mm
French Knot

med purple 4mm
French Knot

med purple 4mm
med dk orchid 4mm
Straight Stitches

med purple 4mm
med dk orchid 4mm
Ribbon Stitches

med yellow-green floss
Backstitch

yellow floss
Colonial Knot

med yellow-green 7mm
Ribbon Stitch

blue floss
Colonial Knot

lt yellow-green 4mm
Straight Stitch

lt gold 4mm
Straight Stitch

Stitching order:

Weave trellis with long, evenly spaced stitches; use floss to work a French Knot at each intersection.

Work Ribbon Stitch leaves on trellis vine. Use floss to Backstitch vine and all stems; work a stitch into the base of each vine leaf. Work remaining leaves with Ribbon Stitch or Straight Stitch.

For each vine rose, work a Spiral Rose. For the tulips, work three overlapping Ribbon Stitches. For the forget-me-nots, use floss to work Colonial Knot petals and centers. For the delphinium blossoms, work Ribbon Stitches near base and Straight Stitches and French Knots near top of each stem in a random color arrangement.

For the butterfly, use floss to Straight Stitch the body and antennae, and work a Colonial Knot for head and French Knots at ends of antennae. Work Straight Stitch wings.

Tulip Family Portrait

(see photo, page 20)

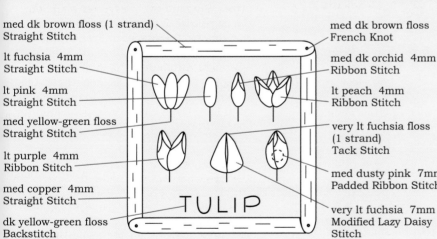

med dk brown floss (1 strand)
Straight Stitch

lt fuchsia 4mm
Straight Stitch

lt pink 4mm
Straight Stitch

med yellow-green floss
Straight Stitch

lt purple 4mm
Ribbon Stitch

med copper 4mm
Straight Stitch

dk yellow-green floss
Backstitch

med dk brown floss
French Knot

med dk orchid 4mm
Ribbon Stitch

lt peach 4mm
Ribbon Stitch

very lt fuchsia floss
(1 strand)
Tack Stitch

med dusty pink 7mm
Padded Ribbon Stitch

very lt fuchsia 7mm
Modified Lazy Daisy
Stitch

TULIP

Stitching order:

Use floss to Straight Stitch stems and Backstitch lettering.

Work tulips with Straight Stitch, Ribbon Stitch, Modified Lazy Daisy, or Padded Ribbon Stitch (two Ribbon Stitches over one Colonial Knot).

For the frame, work long Straight Stitches; use floss to anchor each side with random Straight Stitches, adding a French Knot at each corner.

Violet Border

(see photo, page 19)

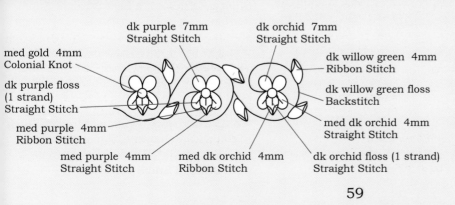

med gold 4mm
Colonial Knot

dk purple floss
(1 strand)
Straight Stitch

med purple 4mm
Ribbon Stitch

med purple 4mm
Straight Stitch

dk purple 7mm
Straight Stitch

dk orchid 7mm
Straight Stitch

dk willow green 4mm
Ribbon Stitch

dk willow green floss
Backstitch

med dk orchid 4mm
Straight Stitch

med dk orchid 4mm
Ribbon Stitch

dk orchid floss (1 strand)
Straight Stitch

Stitching order:

Use floss to Backstitch vine. Work Ribbon Stitch leaves. For upper petals, work Straight Stitches. For lower petals, work two outside Straight Stitches covered with a centered Ribbon Stitch. Work a Colonial Knot at center of each violet. Use floss to Straight Stitch on top of lower petals.

Note: This design can be repeated to form a continuous border.

Violet Bouquet

(see photo, back cover)

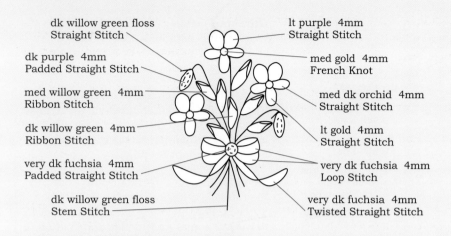

dk willow green floss
Straight Stitch

dk purple 4mm
Padded Straight Stitch

med willow green 4mm
Ribbon Stitch

dk willow green 4mm
Ribbon Stitch

very dk fuchsia 4mm
Padded Straight Stitch

dk willow green floss
Stem Stitch

lt purple 4mm
Straight Stitch

med gold 4mm
French Knot

med dk orchid 4mm
Straight Stitch

lt gold 4mm
Straight Stitch

very dk fuchsia 4mm
Loop Stitch

very dk fuchsia 4mm
Twisted Straight Stitch

Stitching order:
Use floss to Stem Stitch stems. Work Ribbon Stitch leaves.

For each full violet, work Straight Stitch petals and a French Knot at center. For each bud, work a Padded Straight Stitch (Straight Stitch over Straight Stitch); use floss to Straight Stitch calyx.

For bow, work Twisted Straight Stitch streamers, Loop Stitch loops, and a Padded Straight Stitch (Straight Stitch over Straight Stitch) knot.

Williamsburg Garland

(see photo, back cover)

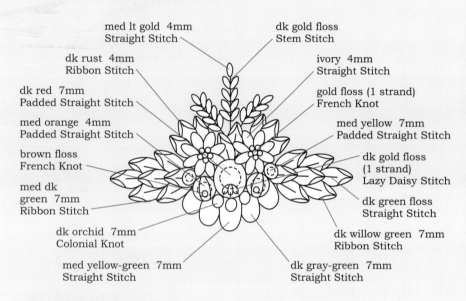

med lt gold 4mm
Straight Stitch

dk rust 4mm
Ribbon Stitch

dk red 7mm
Padded Straight Stitch

med orange 4mm
Padded Straight Stitch

brown floss
French Knot

med dk
green 7mm
Ribbon Stitch

dk orchid 7mm
Colonial Knot

med yellow-green 7mm
Straight Stitch

dk gold floss
Stem Stitch

ivory 4mm
Straight Stitch

gold floss (1 strand)
French Knot

med yellow 7mm
Padded Straight Stitch

dk gold floss
(1 strand)
Lazy Daisy Stitch

dk green floss
Straight Stitch

dk willow green 7mm
Ribbon Stitch

dk gray-green 7mm
Straight Stitch

Stitching order:
Work Ribbon Stitch side leaves; begin at outside edge and overlap leaves, working toward center. Use floss to Straight Stitch a midrib on each leaf. Work Straight Stitch lower leaves. Use floss to Stem Stitch gold branches at back. Work Straight Stitch leaves on branches.

Work Ribbon Stitch leaves at back. For ivory poinsettias, work Straight Stitch petals; use floss to work French Knots at center. Work Padded Straight Stitch (Straight Stitch over Colonial Knot) lemons, oranges, and pomegranate. Use floss to add French Knots to orange ends and Lazy Daisy Stitches to pomegranate base. Work Colonial Knot plums.

Witch & Friends

(see photo, page 20)

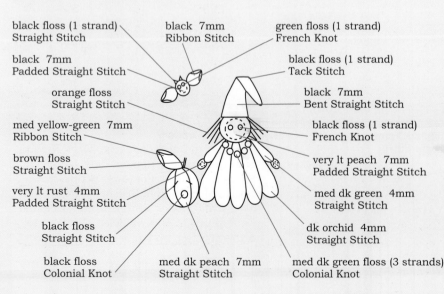

black floss (1 strand)
Straight Stitch

black 7mm
Padded Straight Stitch

orange floss
Straight Stitch

med yellow-green 7mm
Ribbon Stitch

brown floss
Straight Stitch

very lt rust 4mm
Padded Straight Stitch

black floss
Straight Stitch

black floss
Colonial Knot

black 7mm
Ribbon Stitch

med dk peach 7mm
Straight Stitch

green floss (1 strand)
French Knot

black floss (1 strand)
Tack Stitch

black 7mm
Bent Straight Stitch

black floss (1 strand)
French Knot

very lt peach 7mm
Padded Straight Stitch

med dk green 4mm
Straight Stitch

dk orchid 4mm
Straight Stitch

med dk green floss (3 strands)
Colonial Knot

Stitching order:
Work Straight Stitch arms and then dress. Work Padded Straight Stitch (Straight Stitch over Colonial Knot) for head and hands. Use floss to Straight Stitch hair and work French Knot eyes and Colonial Knot beads. Work a Bent Straight Stitch for hat.

For pumpkin, work three overlapping Straight Stitches and a Ribbon Stitch leaf. Use floss to Straight Stitch eyes and stem and work a Colonial Knot mouth.

For the bat, work a Padded Straight Stitch (Straight Stitch over Colonial Knot) body and Ribbon Stitch wings. Use floss for Straight Stitch ears and French Knot eyes.